An
Alternative View On

CRYSTAL HEALING

oOo

Revealing "Power for Life's"
Secret Ingredient

By
ROBERT W. WOOD D.HP
(Diploma in Hypnotherapy)

Rosewood Publishing

First Published in U.K. 2012
by Rosewood Publishing
P.O. Box 219, Huddersfield,
West Yorkshire HD2 2YT
UK

www.rosewood-gifts.co.uk

Robert W Wood D.Hp
asserts the moral right to be identified
as the Author of this work

Copy-editing
Margaret Wakefield BA (Hons) London
www.euroreportage.co.uk

Cover designed by Robert W Wood D.Hp

Cover photograph by
Andrew Caveney BA (Hons)
www.andrewcaveneyphotography.co.uk

ISBN 978-0-9567913-2-0   BK13

Introduction

It's truly believed by many, that Gemstones and Crystals have amazing, magical like, often mysterious and hidden powers.

For thousands of years, people have been telling extraordinary stories about these mysterious powers. Powers which many believe can change their Luck, improve their Health, Wealth, and bring about a Peace of Mind and provide them with abundant Energy.

Is there any proof to support these strange, mysterious stories or are they just Myths, Tales and Legends, that should remain forever buried in the depths of time?

After many years of research, that have led me on to giving numerous talks, presentations and displays in front of thousands of people on this very subject, I now know, beyond any shadow of doubt, that there is good reason to believe these "stories" are in fact quite true.

To give you, the reader, a greater depth of knowledge and understanding with regard to these mysteries that surround Gemstones and Crystals, this book is a record of my research extending over many years and based on my many presentations.

The first part of this book explores the long established connection between Gemstones and Crystals with Astrology. The second part looks at the many various 'Healing' properties of Gemstones and Crystals, and in the final part, I explain what unites the first two parts and just how the 'Healing' properties, with the help of a 'Secret Ingredient', actually work.

Thankfully, what is known as 'Esoteric', that is: Secret or Mysterious, is gradually finding acceptance amongst a new generation of Scientists and Psychologists, who realise that the human experience cannot be explained by scientific proof alone. Who would not be impressed at man's ability to land on the moon, send probes to Mars and beyond?

Yet it remains a fact that if you asked a nuclear physicist how to resolve a moral dilemma, they would probably suggest you looked elsewhere for the answer because they couldn't help.

As with Crystal Healing, science seems unable to help us. Of course, Crystal Healing belongs to that category of phenomena without form, substance or colour. It is not susceptible to investigation by external means but that doesn't mean that it doesn't exist; merely that science can't explain it.

Here's a question: would you be impressed if I said, 'by using a touch of mystery, by revealing a 'Secret Formula', by showing you a deeply hidden essential ingredient, one that once it has been revealed and understood will change your life for the better and for ever.?

If I could de-mystify the mysteries and show you beyond any doubt, how to turn your Birthstone into a special powerful Lucky Talisman and at the same time show you how to get your Healing Crystal to become so effective that you will be amazed and astounded by its power. If I told you that all this can be done by you, because you have a 'Power' that's beyond your imagination and then help you to discover it, and then go on to show you how to use it, well! Would you be impressed?

Because this is exactly what I have been doing, quietly and sincerely, for many years with the help of my talks and with stunning effect. So would you be impressed? Because that is exactly what this book is all about.

We normally see this amazing world through our five senses. However there is a "Sixth Sense" which we often experience but seldom talk about and yet it is here that we will start to find many answers.

So my Quest and promise to you, is to …
De-mystify the Mysteries.

Starting with "Why try to predict the future,
when you are the ones who can change it"

Gemstones and Crystals have been associated with Astrology for over 6,000 years. They can form an important link between themselves and Astrology. In the following chapters, I will show you just how important these links can be.

A journey of a thousand miles starts with a single step. Take your first step now and let me guide you through this amazing "Hidden World", which is often called both 'Magical and Mysterious'.

Robert W Wood D.Hp

Imagine this: all the computers in the world,
without exception, need to be connected
to a Power Source if they are to work.

NOW DISCOVER THE SOURCE OF YOUR POWER

PART ONE
"A Secret Knowledge"

The knowledge many of the ancient civilisations had seems to be the very thing that we modern westerners seem to lack and is what we are endlessly seeking. That is, a deep physical and spiritual connection back to the natural energies and cycles of life, the Earth and the Cosmos.

GENESIS ...in the beginning ...

Some years ago I was offered the opportunity of working for one of the largest wholesalers in Europe, who sold fossils, minerals, semi-precious gemstones and crystals. My challenge was to look at fresh ways of marketing these products using agents to sell direct to the public.

Before this my interest in Gemstones and Crystals was zero. However I soon found, very pleasantly, that the whole subject of the mysteries surrounding Gemstones and Crystals was very intriguing. I was looking at designing a range of new gifts, and looking for a novel way of launching this new range. It was at this time, that with a flash of inspiration, someone suggested Birthstones (because there are only 12, aren't there?)

At the time I had no idea of the true connections between Gemstones, Crystals and Astrology and even less idea which Gemstone truly represented each star sign. I quickly realised just how vast this subject was going to be because I had to find exactly which stones, from every corner of the earth, could be called authentic Birthstones.

After months of detailed research, I found that there was a lot more to Gemstones than just their natural aesthetic appeal. Each stone had an identity, a characteristic which through time has been used to promote Beauty, Healing, to ease Stress and used as tokens of Good Luck and Fortune.

My discoveries were very surprising, even if a little unexpected but always exciting because it led me deeper into a subject that I found to be totally absorbing, not only to myself but to a wide range of people, from all kinds of backgrounds. I soon found that giving talks to groups of people (mainly ladies groups) on this interesting subject only led me deeper into its fascination.

The Birth of Civilisation

Our planet Earth is approximately 4,500 million years old, and plants and insects have been around for over 450 million years. Dinosaurs, after ruling the earth for millions of years, finally became extinct 65 million years ago and if you believe in evolution, then man has only been around for 2 or 3 million years, although it has to be said there is still no proof that man has been around for more than a few thousand years.

In pre-historic times, people were nomadic, always on the move from one camp to another, almost like the migrating animals of today. About 6,000 years ago, early man started to settle down and began to build more permanent homes and settlements. He then started keeping animals for food and the fleeces for clothing and developed skills for growing crops to feed his family.

At about the same time, the Babylonians, the Egyptians and the Chinese began to believe that the Stars and other heavenly bodies that they could see so clearly in the night sky influenced the lives of all men.

The Babylonians, in particular, thought that the position of the stars represented coded messages from the gods. Their Priests spent much of their studying these so called messages by observing and plotting the night's sky with great care and detail.

Studying in this way they were able to produce very accurate maps that recorded the position of the stars in relationship to the time of year. They were able to correlate the seasons with the rotation of the Earth, the Moon and the Sun, a science that is now known as Astrology.

With this knowledge, they divided the heavens or the night sky into different regions or areas of various groups of stars. We now know these as Constellations and they named each area after their pagan Gods, Animals and even common objects.

The Signs of the Zodiac

The Sages or High Priests, men who were revered for their profound wisdom and knowledge, apparently knew a great deal about the Dog Star Sirius A and its smaller companion star Sirius B, despite the fact that both these bodies are way outside our own Solar System.

Early man thought that messengers from the star system Sirius descended from the skies onto Earth in order to teach their ancestors good government and to introduce systems for counting and writing. The Dog Star thus became known as the God Star. It was the Greeks that later renamed the constellations after their own gods and thus provided us with the now familiar twelve Signs of the Zodiac.

The Sumerians were probably the first to relate Gemstones to the Planet Earth and the Solar System. They were already cutting and polishing softer Gemstones such as Rock Crystal, Amethyst and Agates. They were using them extensively to decorate their buildings and artefacts, to add splendour and majesty. Members of Royal families also wore Gemstones set in silver, as jewellery as a sign of status.

Originally they probably used simply the colour of each stone, as the link with the various Constellations. The Greeks believed that Gemstones like humans were born under the influence of the planets. An example: a person born under the sign of Pisces shared that sign with the Gemstone Amethyst. Birthstones were originally given to a new born child maybe in the form of a pendant or a loose stone, so as to protect the child from harm and help attract and bring about good fortune.

Which Twelve Birthstones?

From the outset, the quest was to find twelve Authentic Birthstones. Initially I found that there was a huge amount of conflicting evidence on exactly which Birthstones were used, although this may have been explained by the lack of local availability or variations because of personal preferences.

To find an answer, I carefully studied many different Birthstone lists published by world famous Astrologers. I read with great interest articles in several encyclopaedias and studied the Old and New Testaments. I consulted various New Age Publications, in fact any relevant article in books and magazines. In many cases the lists varied amazingly far and wide so what I initially decided to do, was to take the 'mean average'. If the majority named Red Jasper as the birthstone for Aries, then that was good enough for me and that's how I got my list of twelve.

So using this method of the mean average, I was able to select my Twelve Birthstones and my final selection became:-

> Aries ....Red Jasper
> Taurus ....Rose Quartz
> Gemini ....Black Onyx
> Cancer ....Mother of Pearl
> Leo ....Tiger Eye
> Virgo ....Carnelian
> Libra ....Green Aventurine
> Scorpio ......Rhodonite
> Sagittarius .Sodalite
> Capricorn ...Obsidian Snowflake
> Aquarius ....Blue Onyx
> Pisces ....Amethyst

These lists have now been heavily researched and although there are other lists, this is my list and I now believe it to be as authentic as any other list.

Birthstones … Semi Precious or Precious?

It became apparent very early on in my research that today's high value Birthstones were never used by any ancient civilisation. That is not to say that these stones were not known. We know though, that these high value stones were far too hard for the ancient civilisations to polish with their primitive techniques. So it was softer semi-precious Gemstones that became regarded as valuable. The exotic jewellery found in the Pyramids and at major archaeological digs including ancient burial grounds supports this.

Faceting or the cutting and polishing of the hardest, high value Gemstones was not made possible until around the sixteenth century, when a German jeweller first perfected the process. Not surprisingly the trend caught on. People preferred the highly faceted and radiantly polished stones that could produce such brilliance by 'reflected light from within'. Not only were these Gemstones aesthetically more beautiful but they became a symbol of refinement and wealth.

It was at the turn of the twentieth century that the present Birthstone lists were created by large Dutch and English Diamond Houses, merely in order to promote the sale of their 'high value' Gemstones. Obviously there are more profits to be made from retailing Diamonds and other high value stones, than those made by selling today's semi-precious stones.

The claims that high value gemstones of today's world are 'authentic birthstones' must be treated as highly doubtful.

Birthstones … yes, but are they the right ones?

So I had my list of twelve Birthstones. I then decided to look further into the different stories, myths and beliefs, that they could have an influence or positive impact on our lives. One explanation is that our bodies reverberate to celestial vibrations and that throughout our lives we have this 'vibration' of our ruling planets within our bodies. Never is this planetary influence so strong, as at the time we are born.

Using the appropriate birthstone seems to contribute to putting us closer in line with the energies of our astrological sign and its ruling planet. It also appears that the beneficial action of these stones is automatic. It seems that they are working for you however passive you or they seem to be. This action is similar to the moon having an influence over our vast oceans, that is, it produces the tidal effect although the power to do this cannot be seen.

As time goes on we realise that this mysterious process of creation is still going on.

After creating my list of twelve birthstones, I decided to see if there was any connection between people's star signs and the twelve birthstones I was working with. I developed a way of testing to see if there was a connection. I simply put several of each of the twelve birthstones, in the form of small tumble stones, into a basket. Then I past this basket around the various groups and organisations that I was presenting to, and asked them pick out a stone they liked.

The results seemed astounding, really amazing, because I was getting regularly over 50% to 60% of my audience actually picking out their own birthstones but the bigger surprise was this: those that hadn't picked out their own birthstones seemed to be picking out their opposite stones. More on this later as I explain the 'Law of Polarity', however one explanation could simply be that they were picking them out by colour.

A talk at the local Police Station.
I was invited to give a talk at my local Police headquarters. This presentation turned out to be unusual for two reasons. First of all there were 36 ladies present, in what was the CID lounge. All were either retired police officers or ladies who were married to police offices, with the exception of one lady who was in uniform. She was acting as a liaison officer for the group. At the start of my talks I often ask everybody, by a show of hands, for their star sign. Now over the years I

have discovered that wherever a group of people get together and I asked them their star signs a pattern seems to emerge. That is, if there are 24 in the room then there is a good chance that there will be two of each of the star signs in the room. If there are 48 then there is a good chance that they are still equally represented and that there would be four of each star sign there in the room. It's not always true but seems to happen so often that it leads me to believe it may be normal. In other words wherever a group of people get together and you get the chance to ask them their star signs you will find more often than not a pattern emerging.

I was telling this story to this group of retired officers and went on to suggest that because they were linked by a profession it probably wouldn't work. So I asked them by a show of hands how many 'Aries' were in the room. Surprisingly three hands went up. How many Taurus and another three hands went up, anybody Gemini and again three hands went up. I couldn't believe it but by this time you could hear a pin drop. I have never seen a room become so quiet with anticipation when I had finished I had ten threes a two and a four that's as close to perfect I have ever got. There was quite an unusual atmosphere, an odd feeling about that morning.

Remember a Mystery is no longer a mystery,
When you know how it works

The other thing that made this display so memorable was this: I always finish my presentations with a free raffle and I give away a free £5 gift voucher to the winner. When I called out the winning number 54 nobody responded. I could see everybody and then I said to a lady at the back of the room "You have won this", then she found her ticket, the number 54 and said "How did you know that, you must be a mystic a psychic!" Well I am not, at least I don't think I am. I never did tell her how I knew it was her; in fact I left her thinking I could read her mind. I'll tell you how I knew, I had called out this number and nobody had said a word then I caught a glimpse of this woman looking into her handbag at the back of the room, as quick as a flash I realised if it wasn't anybody else it had to be her.

Sometimes people do see things differently and it may be simply because they have a better view.

6,000 years ago, ancient man had knowledge
That today's modern man is only just rediscovering

The Law of Polarity, the Opposite Star Signs

During my research I came across this 'Law of Polarity'. This states that everything has an opposite – for example night and day, hot and cold, right and wrong, up and down, ying and yang etc. etc. In astrology it means the opposite star sign becomes very important. That is, the meaning of one is enhanced by the knowledge of the other. If you read your horoscope, why not in future, for fun, read both your own and your opposite star sign. It may help you to gain a much fuller picture.

If you imagine your own star sign as representing you – the 'you' others can see – then your opposite is representative of your inner world, a world others can't see. A world from within; your inner thoughts; a world only you can visit. Finally, and this is amazing, as we go through mid-life we 'flip' over to the opposite side. It's called 'The Law of Polarity' and it's featured in every birth chart, and it shows each sign of the zodiac as having its own 'polar' opposite. For example, if your star sign is Aries, then your opposite sign is Libra and if you were Libra your opposite would be Aries. Try it, next time you are reading your horoscope, why not for fun, read your opposite.

Listed below is each star sign along with its opposite:-
Aries is opposite Libra and Libra is opposite Aries.
Taurus is opposite Scorpio and Scorpio is opposite Taurus.
Gemini is opposite Sagittarius and Sagittarius is opposite Gemini.
Cancer is opposite Capricorn and Capricorn is opposite Cancer.
Leo is opposite Aquarius and Aquarius is opposite Leo.
Virgo is opposite Pisces and Pisces is opposite Virgo.

Gemstones and the Bible

In the early days of my research some friends told me that the gemstones and crystals that I was researching could be found in the Bible. When I enquired where in the Bible, the answer came back that they didn't have a clue where, they just knew that they were there. Because of my research and new found interest, I wanted to see if I could find them.

Now imagine this, there are no home PCs and I hadn't heard of a 'Concordance' (this is a guide that helps you to find your way around a Bible). I managed to get hold of a Bible and it had almost 1,400 pages in it, *I only knew because I looked at the last page.* It was a Thursday morning and I started to think "how would you find these stones in the Bible?" – when something strange seemed to happen; the book seemed to open up and on the page I was drawn to a lovely story in Exodus.

Exodus 28:15 the Breastpiece

It's all about God asking Aaron – Moses' brother, who will become the first High Priest – to fashion a 'Breastpiece'. And on this 'Breastpiece' God instructed him to place twelve stones, saying that these twelve stones would represent the twelve tribes of Israel.

I thought, 'This is symbolism.' In Astrology, twelve stones represent the cycle of life and are called Birthstones. However, within hours on the same day, I was drawn to another page. This was in the New Testament (Rev. 21–19) where it talks about a New Jerusalem; and there's another list of twelve stones. Now this list is different from the first, but this second list is very interesting because Red Jasper, which by using the mean average I had chosen to represent Aries in Astrology, was the first foundation for the New Jerusalem in the Scriptures.

So, being curious, I read on, only to find that the sixth foundation for the New Jerusalem was Carnelian – and Carnelian was the birthstone I had picked for Virgo, the sixth sign in Astrology. The twelfth foundation was Amethyst – and Amethyst was the same gemstone I had picked for Pisces, the twelfth sign.

Later, after using other references, computers and concordances, I realised that on that same day I had found. or had I been shown, the only two places in the whole of the Old and New Testaments of the Bible, where there are lists of twelve stones. On reflection the whole experience seemed so strange looking back on it and yet it must have been meant.

Pisces the Fish

My research brought up another surprise when I discovered an unusual connection with the zodiac sign of Pisces and Christianity.

The Astrological sign for Pisces is represented by a sign of a fish.

It also represents the final energy of the cycle of life, a unifying energy, before it goes back to Aries. But in Astrology Pisces is also known as a sign of a 'healer'. In the early days of Christianity the Romans persecuted them, so they developed a secret sign; they would draw half the sign of the fish in the sand to identify themselves to strangers. If the stranger completed the mirror image of the fish, they then both knew that they were followers of Jesus Christ.

What an interesting way of describing Jesus, using a symbol that was probably born out of knowledge found four thousand years earlier in Astrology. Could this explain why the earliest Christians used a fish as their secret sign?

For hundreds of years the Fish remained a secret, covert symbol of Christ. In the fourth century the Cross was to take over as the major Christian symbol. With the growing popularity of the cross came the decline in the use of the ancient fish symbol.

In the 20th century 'Born Again' Christians were looking for an alternative Christian symbol that was more personal and less associated with the Church. They adopted the ancient fish, and since then it has once again become one of the best known Christian symbols. Today we can see many cars which display this symbol, which is now being used once again to represent the Christian faith.

A Methodist story

Many years ago I was giving a talk at a Methodist church, and when I had finished one of the elders came and told me a little story about their Minister. He had gone to Blackpool for the day and for lunch he had bought fish and chips. He was served with the biggest fish imaginable and so he made a complimentary remark about the size of his portion to the gentleman who had served him. "We look after our own," he said, "we noticed," looking at the symbol of a fish on his lapel, "you're in the Fish Fryers Association".

I thought this was a great joke until I discovered it wasn't, because The Fish Fryers Association does exist and yes the same symbol of a fish is their logo.

Some further Biblical references linked to Astrology

ISAIAH 47:13 all the council you have received has only worn you out! Let your Astrologers come forward, those stargazers who make predictions month by month let them save you from what is coming upon you.

NUMBERS 24:17 I see him, but not now; I behold him, but not near. A star will come out of Jacob.

DANIEL 2:27 Daniel replied, No wise man, enchanter, magician or diviner can explain to the King, the mystery he has asked about.
2:28 but there is a God in heaven who reveals mysteries. He has shown King Nebuchadnezzar what will happen in the days to come. Your dream and the visions that passed through your mind as you lay on your bed are these.

Signs of the end of the Age
LUKE 21:25 There will be signs in the sun, moon and stars.

The visit of the Magi
MATTHEW 2:2-3 After Jesus was born in Bethlehem in Judea, during the time of King Herod, Magi from the east came to Jerusalem and asked, where is the one who has been born King of the Jews? We saw his star in the east and have come to worship him.

We have all heard the story of the 'Three Wise Men'. It is generally believed that they were very able Astronomers. In 5BC there was a Stella Nova, an exploding star, and this could be seen quite clearly in the clear night sky. Under ancient Astrological beliefs, this meant a new beginning involving Royalty to the Jews. Three conjunctions or the close proximity of planets, as seen from Earth, all occurring within a period of six months all enhanced the importance of the event.

Everyone saw these celestial happenings, and the Astrological interpretations were universal at the time. Using modern technology and Astrological knowledge and using powerful computers it is now estimated that these events did all take place in the year 5BC. Using the combined knowledge it's been suggested that the birth of Jesus Christ was in fact 7th of May 5BC. That would make him a Taurus, giving Jesus, like the Queen, two birthdays, the official one and his actual one.

We can see the effect of the stars in the skies
But we can't see what scattered them

We can see and feel the rays of the Sun
But we can't see the power that created it.

A Scientific Approach

In time, with the help and guidance, we are slowly learning to see the unseen, we are starting to hear that which cannot be heard and are finding ways of speaking the unspoken. Today's scientists have demonstrated a solid connection between the position of the solar system at the time of one's birth and the subsequent success of an individual's career. They have also found a connection between the planets and the traits associated with character and personality of people under the sign of each planet.

Michael Gauquelin (1928–1991), a French psychologist, analysed thousands of birth charts. He found that the very best in various fields of excellence were all associated with the same time of year in which they were born. In France, they record not only the date of birth but also the time, unlike the U.K. where the actual time is only recorded in the case of multiple births; because of this, he was able to conduct a very accurate study.

From his work and the detailed results, it is strange to think that it is possible that by just simply asking someone their date and time of birth, plus three or four further questions, he could produce a very accurate 'Personal Psychological Profile'. We can use his methods today to find our own or an associate's personal profile.

Psychological Profiles

Although we are not exactly sure how Astrology works, it doesn't stop us from using it. The ancient mariners used a compass with amazing results for hundreds of years, circumnavigating all around the world, and they had no idea why their compass worked. They were not so worried about how it worked but relied entirely on the fact that it did.

Now if you take away the more contentious prediction side of Astrology, the flamboyant type of 'mystics' as well as the 'entertainers' and the 'weirdoes', then what you have left, are interesting facts and theories which just cannot be dismissed or ignored. The modern view is that the planets that are moving in a predictable cycle, for reasons still unknown seem to mirror the influences which affect us all, especially in relationships to our characters and personalities.

Imagine the twelve signs of the zodiac as a symbolic representation of expressions of energy, as if the life force, symbolised by the planets, is diffused and refracted to express every conceivable behavioural characteristic associated with 'Man'; for example: just as light being directed through a prism is diffused into all the colours of the rainbow. Astrology seems to have helped give birth to what we now know as a psychological profile.

There's no doubt that a new age for Astrology has begun, which raises the question of whether Astrology does stand as a practical source of information. In psychotherapy, it can certainly prove to be a very useful way of showing great insight into 'Personality'.

In 1911, Carl Gustav Jung (pronounced Young) published his work on the 'Psychology of the Unconscious'. Until then he had been a leading collaborator with Sigmund Freud. Carl Jung was a Swiss psychotherapist, and he believed that two years of therapy would be needed, to give him the same insight that could be produced from an "in depth birth chart".

He was certainly considered an expert in his chosen field and believed that a skilled 'Birth Chart' could contain over two thousand times more information than say any ordinary 'star sign' Horoscope found in today's modern magazines or newspapers. Carl Jung, along with Freud, was the main influences on the twentieth century's fascination with the mind, and in particular the 'unconscious mind'.

For reasons already explained, it seems that the 'time' of birth and the placement of the planets at the time of birth can tell a skilled Astrologer much about an individual's talents. They are able to analyse their hang-ups, their temperament and more astonishingly their psychological make-up, all from the knowledge of the date and time of birth.

Although not openly talked about, it's widely believed that even modern political leaders or their wives as well as many business entrepreneurs are known to have used 'Astrology' for much of their decision-making regarding problems. However we are still learning to what extent contemporary political leaders are involved in using Astrology.

In the Middle East and India, leaders openly use Astrologers along with a host of other advisers. As Astrology becomes increasingly simple to understand, its place in Government may become a far more familiar sight and a far greater source of information. It is interesting to note that up to the seventeenth century political, Astrology had a respected image and place in the eyes of the rich and powerful. Its many practitioners ran from the Roman Emperor Tiberius to the time of the English Civil War in the 1640s, where William Lilly, the great court Astrologer, amazingly advised both Oliver Cromwell and his adversary Charles 1st at the same time.

Psychological profiles used for commercial use
In today's competitive world, just imagine if you were able to know all you needed to know about any person, even before you ever met them, especially before you had to interview them for a position of employment. With this knowledge, you would certainly appreciate the benefits and the tremendous advantages that this sort of information would give you. Modern business is already paying small fortunes to outside recruitment agencies to provide this knowledge and so find the most appropriate candidate for their vacancies. Many companies already use psychological profile tests in their first appraisal of candidates for a vacancy. The era of the C.V. alone is far from being the only method now known for selecting suitable employees.

Candidates are often asked questions without them fully realising what exactly is behind that question. There is often no right or wrong answer to these questions but your reply will help them to see exactly your outlook and understanding of a vast number of topics. How you see things, how you make decisions, if you would fit into their team and certainly whether or not you were suitable for the position.

They are able to decide from this information, whether you would be suitable or not, even before you had the chance of an interview. If you did manage to pass their psychological tests, then the interview may just be a matter of formality. These tests and profiles can be well over 90% accurate. For those that find Astrology interesting, it seems it can provide a solid base for complete analysis, If the present pace of change continues then perhaps Astrology will gain a very credible image in this New Millennium.

Even the Church use a similar system known as the "Myer's Briggs Typology". They have discovered that by using this kind of system, they can identify and separate a person's physical from the spiritual.

A humorous little piece – the author is unknown.
Why did Jesus choose these twelve?
Memo
To: Jesus, son of Joseph. Joiners workshop, Woodcraft Street, Nazareth.
From: The Jordan Management Consultant Co. Jerusalem.
Subject: A staff 'Aptitude Evaluation'

Thank you for submitting the resumes of the twelve men you have picked for management positions in your new organisation. All of them have now taken our battery of tests and we have not only run the results through our computer but also arranged personal interviews for each of them with our psychologist and vocational consultant. It is a staff opinion that most of your nominees are lacking in background education and vocational aptitude for the type of enterprise you are undertaking.

We would recommend that you continue your search for persons of experience and managerial ability and proven capability.

Simon Peter is emotionally unstable and given to fits of temper. Andrew has absolutely no qualities of leadership. The two brothers, James and John, the sons of Zebedee, will place personal interest above any company loyalty. Thomas demonstrates a questioning attitude that would tend to undermine morale. We feel it is our duty to tell you that Mathew has been blacklisted by the Greater Jerusalem Better Business Bureau. James the son of Alpheus and Thaddeus definitely has radical leanings and they both registered a high score on the manic depressive scale.

One of the candidates however shows great potential. He's a man of ability and resourcefulness, meets people well, has a keen business mind and has contacts in high places. He is highly motivated, ambitious and innovative. We recommend Judas Iscariot as your controller and right hand man. All other profiles are self-explanatory.

We wish you every success in your new venture.

The first newspaper Astrological column was published in the Sunday Express, when R.H. Naylor wrote a brief feature to commemorate the birth of Princess Margaret on the 24th of August 1930. This became the forerunner of our modern daily Horoscopes that appear so regularly in newspapers and magazines.

Fire, Earth, Air and Water

Another division of the Zodiac is the grouping of three otherwise unrelated Zodiac Signs under one of four basic fundamental natures. These are collectively known as the 'Elements', and each Zodiac sign associated with the same 'Element' shares numerous common characteristics.

The 'Elements' allow us to gain rapid insight into the manner in which we perceive life and so to help our psychological profiles further; so the 'Elements' have been included.

It is also interesting to note Jung's understanding and association of the Elements with Jungian functions: Intuition (Fire); Sensation (Earth); Thinking (Air) and Feeling (Water). A number of able Astrologers and those with knowledge and experience of the concepts involved with Astrology and Jungian analytical psychology have had varying degrees of success with linking the two together.

In my book 'Astrology: the Secret Code" you will find the different psychological traits, both negative and positive characteristics and personalities associated with the different Star Signs of the Zodiac; and don't forget the "Law of Polarity", that is: 'The meaning of one is enhanced by the knowledge of the other'. So in future, if you read your horoscopes don't forget to read your opposite star sign, to gain a fuller picture. Although my book 'Astrology: the Secret Code" contains much more detail, here is a little sampler:-

Aries and Libra are opposites ....

ARIES ... Birthstone Red Jasper ... Arians have a straightforward and positive attitude to life. They need adventure and like to take risks. Positive traits: courageous, enthusiastic, independent and forthright. Negative traits; extravagant, impulsive, brash and impatient.

LIBRA ... Birthstone Green Aventurine ... This is the sign of fair play and harmony. Librans are charmers who enjoy socialising and do not like to feel left out. Positive traits: gracious, cheerful, charming and refined. Negative traits: manipulative, procrastinating, indecisive.

" Why try to predict the future, when you are the one that can change it"

Taurus and Scorpio are opposites ...

TAURUS ... Birthstone Rose Quartz ... Taureans are very loyal, sensible and reliable but need security and routine in their lives. Positive traits: sincere, reliable, stable and faithful. Negative traits: obsessive, intransigent, possessive and naïve.

SCORPIO ... Birthstone Rhodonite ... Scorpios are energetic, intense, sensual people. They enjoy positions of power and are very searching. Positive traits: resourceful, decisive, persuasive and focused. Negative traits: resentful, vindictive, sarcastic and suspicious.

Gemini and Sagittarius are opposites ...

GEMINI ... Birthstone Black Onyx ... Very chatty, lively people who make good salespeople with a natural ability to sell. Positive traits: humorous, witty, versatile communicative and spontaneous. Negative traits: emotionally detached, flighty, restless and fickle,

SAGITTARIUS ... Birthstone Sodalite ... The hunters who need freedom and stimulation, fun loving with a thirst for knowledge. Positive traits: frank, logical, kind generous and honest. Negative traits: extravagant, quarrelsome, blunt and irresponsible.

Cancer and Capricorn are opposites ...

CANCER ... Birthstone Mother of Pearl ... Cancerians are very nice, caring and sensitive, with a tendency to worry. Positive traits: industrious, thrifty, loyal, sensitive and tenacious. Negative traits: secretive, cloying, touchy and clinging.

CAPRICORN ... Birthstone Obsidian Snowflake ... Capricorns are ambitious, hard-working, independent individuals who enjoy good taste. Positive traits; profound, patient, practical, efficient and hard-working. Negative traits: gloomy, snobbish, materialistic and intolerant.

Leo and Aquarius are opposites.

LEO ... Birthstone Tiger Eye ... Leos are leaders and organisers who love life. They are generous and like to spend. Positive traits: benevolent, hospitable, forgiving, affectionate and forgiving. Negative traits: self-centred, vain, gullible and domineering.

AQUARIUS ... Birthstone Blue Onyx ... Aquarians make excellent friends as they are understanding and faithful. They are complex characters, original and magnetic. Positive traits: trustworthy, caring, intuitive, friendly and broad-minded. Negative traits: moody, rebellious, stubborn, abrupt and impersonal.

Virgo and Pisces are opposites.

VIRGO ... Birthstone Carnelian ... Virgos are workers, practical and neat in every way. They can be perfectionists and critical. Positive traits: studious, considerate, discriminating and analytical. Negative traits: prone to worry, detached, sceptical and cynical.

PISCES ... Birthstone Amethyst ... Pisceans are creative and imaginative but sometimes lack confidence. They are very caring, sensitive, kind characters. Positive traits: unassuming, courteous, artistic imaginative and lenient. Negative traits: apologetic, irrational, changeable and self-pitying.

"Anybody who still thinks the sky is the limit
is short of imagination"

From the beginning of time, man has tried to explain the many mysteries of life, its origins and purpose using stories, prophecies, sorcery, myths and legends. We have to accept that man was given, or was he guided to the 'Secret Ingredient', a kind of 'key'. It's a 'key' that has given understanding and although this understanding or knowledge has been cloaked deep in the mysteries of time, it seems that with the aid of our imagination, we are now just beginning to understand its power.

Negative traits

Watch out for those negative traits; nobody likes them – and that includes me and I am writing this. These negative traits are not a 'dark' side but a kind of inner strength; it's what gives us the confidence when we need it. Imagine having a gun and under certain circumstances it may give you confidence, but you don't have to shoot it. Think of what Bob Geldof had to go through to get Band Aid off the ground and then you can see just how useful these traits can be.

I remember at one of my talks, I overheard a woman telling her friend, after she had read out the negative traits for her 'son-in-law': "You know this has got him to a 'T', I'm not surprised she's getting divorced. I told her not to marry him." Generally speaking you won't recognise the negative traits in anyone unless they are ill or life is really being hard on them. I remember saying to my wife, "You know these negative traits are wrong, they are nothing like me." She shouted back, "When you're in a mood, Robert..." so I didn't say any more.

And Finally for Astrology ...

Some friendly advice: do not be so easily taken in, do not eagerly accept another person's interpretations and predictions because if you realised the power that you have, you would not be in such a hurry to give it away. If you do, you are neglecting the refinement and the trust of your own convictions, your inner resources and your proper capacities for decision making, your 'free will' and your instinct. The Church has a very simple view on all this: "Why dabble with a poor substitute, when you can have the real thing? Why dabble with an inferior power, when you can go straight to the HEAD."

To summarize ...

So the modern view of Astrology is this, that it is only a reflection of 'Life', not mystical or magical, only natural. Astrology in a way is just like a mirror; looking into it doesn't make anything happen.

By looking at Astrology in this uncomplicated way, we are then able to use the information freely and in this way, still control our own 'Free Will'; removing any hostility or mysticism away from Astrology gives 'Free Will' back to where it belongs, within the individual.

Many ancient beliefs have been revalidated as science has stepped in to explain the links between the planets and ourselves, whilst showing stones for what they may be, 'Mediators' between the 'Hidden Power', the Earth and ourselves. Birthstones therefore connect the individual, esoterically, with the 'Cosmos', and by using as yet unknown powers, they can help to attract Health, Wealth, Happiness and Success. The role of this book is no more than that of a signpost. Follow the directions life has indicated. However, it is always wise to test every step of the way in the light of your own experiences, for the essential point is to find out for yourself your personal journey, your mission in life.

There is a famous book of Magical Law reputed to have been written by King Solomon over three thousand years ago, which is said to be so powerful, that it should only be used with the "Wisdom of Solomon".

WISDOM. PROVERBS 8. 17:21

I love those who love me.
And those who seek me find me.
With me are riches and honour,
Enduring wealth and prosperity.
My fruit is better than fine gold,
What I yield surpasses choice silver.
I walk in the way of righteousness,
Along the paths of justice.
Bestowing wealth on those who love me,
And making their treasuries full.

PART TWO

Awaken to a glorious world of 'Mystery'.
By looking into your heart you will find the truth,
who you are, what is right and what is not, always remembering
that beauty and goodness exist in everything.

Healing Gemstones and Crystals
In the previous section on 'Astrology', I have shown just how ancient civilisations were searching for knowledge of the Universe. I named twelve birthstones, the ones that I believe to be authentic, and have showed the connection between various gemstones and the astrological signs of the Zodiac. Whilst researching into the 'value of birthstones' I repeatedly came across references to the 'healing properties' of gemstones and crystals.

The 'Sages', very often the High Priests, who were revered for their profound wisdom and great knowledge, were also regarded as the 'medical practitioners' of their time. Without the use of our modern day drugs and knowledge, they had to discover and use more 'Natural' remedies for healing the sick.

Their amazing skills must have seemed astounding to the 'layman', especially at a time of so little education. They had to rely completely on natural elements to effect their cures and help to bring relief from pain and injury. We know for certain that they used a wide range of Herbs and Plants for certain ailments. They also used the Oils from certain plants as cures, the same Oils we now know today as Aromatherapy. They were also aware of the value of certain Minerals, which could be found locally or traded with the wandering nomads.

It's also well documented that the 'Sages' widely used a whole range of Gemstones and Crystals to bring about effective cures. These cures were using 'Holistic healing techniques', and regularly achieved spectacular successes.

The Priests somehow knew that Gemstones and Crystals, many of them being the same ones associated with the star signs, could bring about, amongst other things, great benefits to the health and welfare of their people. They had knowledge and wisdom that they used so skilfully that they could treat a wide range of illnesses and injuries including mental conditions. They used the 'interaction' between the Gemstones and Crystals themselves and the 'belief' that they could in fact bring about a cure.

At the very heart of this interplay, we find that the coming together of these factors became impossible to disconnect or separate, as the bonding of this interplay manifests itself as the 'Cure', and healing naturally commences and then takes place. Today when we are ill, stressed, depressed or just generally run down, we could easily describe our condition as being out of balance with nature. The Priests must have thought that they had discovered one of the greatest 'Secrets of the Universe', when they first discovered that by just being near to a particular Gemstone or Crystal restored the sick back to health. They must have thought that a kind of energy, one that seemed to be transmitted from the stones, was responsible for the favourable reactions.

Holistic Crystal Healers all say that Gemstones and Crystals do have healing properties. So I decided to take a closer look into these claims. Under the title of 'Alternative Therapies' let's explore these claims. I will list some of the most important characteristics of the most popular and easily attainable healing stones. That is the 'Holistic Nature' of these stones, away from their Astrological properties.

Alternative Therapies

All Crystals, Gemstones and Minerals contain trace elements like Iron, Copper, Sodium or Chlorine. Our bodies need these trace elements to function properly. For example, expectant mothers need plenty of Iron.

Babies and growing children need lots of Calcium. We all take regular supplies, without question, of Sodium Chloride or common salt, and take Epsom salts for stomach complaints. We also have Fluoride added to our water whether we like it or not; and these are just a few of the minerals we need and normally take internally. Sometimes these elements are taken in through our skin in the form of creams or oils; we readily administer these daily without any thought of their chemical contents. What do these treatments contain? Mainly some form of natural oil with trace elements of minerals, surprisingly the same minerals commonly found in Gemstones and Crystals.

Over the centuries medical journals have been written, folklore and family traditions have been passed down, and over many years a comprehensive guide would have been available so as to help those that needed help. Early doctors were known as Lapidaries. Lapidaries administered medical treatments very much in the same way as our chemists do today. Certain Gemstones and Crystals were crushed and dispensed to cure many ailments; they were either put on the skin in the form of a 'poultice' or taken internally. It is recorded the Pope Clement V11 who died in 1534 had taken enormous quantities of crushed gemstones to cure his ailments; it's not known however what he actually died of. *(see precautionary warning page 117)*

Copper
It is well known that wearing a Copper bracelet can help to ease arthritic pain and many people will 'swear blind' that it does. In research I actually found plenty of evidence to support these statements. Copper mixes easily with other metals; for example, copper, tin and zinc make bronze. Copper is thought to be one of the best transmitters of healing energy. This idea may be because it was used very successfully against cholera; the Church quickly discovered that men who worked with copper didn't seem to get cholera and so all the Holy men wore large copper discs below their clothes.

They found that wearing copper improved the metabolism, reduced inflammation and increased blood flow. Worn next to the skin it soothes arthritis and rheumatism and can kill all kinds of bacteria. Certain bacteria are found in plenty on silver coins but are never found on copper coins.

So the idea of being cured by a lump of rock may sound crazy, but that is exactly what is being said: that Precious stones and Crystals have been doing just that since the dawn of time. Scientific research seems to help; it has now shown an amazing fact, that Gemstones and Crystals vibrate at different frequencies. For example, a digital watch works because a small piece of pure clear quartz vibrates at a constant frequency when stimulated by the energy from a battery.

Quartz Crystal
There is one simple demonstration of crystal power, which can been seen every day. Have you ever used a special lighter wand to ignite your gas oven or hob? You will be aware of a spark that is created when the wand is squeezed. However, did you know that there is no battery in these devices? In fact the spark is solely created by a small piece of quartz crystal.

Why is there quartz in a watch? The answer is, because quartz makes a timepiece so accurate, to within only a second or two a year – and that's accurate. So how does it work? Scientists discovered that the atoms within a micro-thin slice of synthetic quartz (such as is ideal for clocks and watches) vibrate at 32,768 times per second. The crystal requires very little power, and this is often supplied by a very tiny battery. As the atoms in the quartz vibrate they emit very precise electronic pulses. These pulses are then channelled through microchip circuitry, where they are successively halved in a series of 15 steps. The result is really astounding: it produces a single, constant pulse per second. This is why watches and clocks are now so accurate.

Experts believe that our bodies can act like a watch battery. We can stimulate Crystals in such a way, that they can have a beneficial effect on our wellbeing. It's thought that if we place crystals close to us, our bodies will tune into the vibrating frequency and be energised by them, and healed.

One of the simplest ways to benefit from the power of Crystals is to wear one, or even carry them in a bag or pocket, and then at night place them nearby whilst you sleep. Each Gemstone emits its own unique energy and so it's wise to keep the stone near. The closer they are the greater the benefits.

Thought patterns create energy. Positive thoughts are amplified by using Gemstone Crystals and when these are combined with our body's own natural healing energy they can bring great relief to many conditions. It's worth noting that if you are naturally attracted to any one crystal in particular, then the chances are you will benefit far greater by using that crystal. Some think that it's more the stones finding us, than we finding them.

Once a gemstone or crystal has been found and selected it's a good idea to clean it. This can be done simply by cleaning the stone with clean cool running water and then allowing it to dry naturally in the open air. Some say they should be washed in salt water; so the sea is ideal, but if you're not near to the sea then just add some salt to water. Others believe that gemstones and crystals can attract negative energy from other people, and, again, cleansing is a way of wiping them clean.

Whichever way you decide on, make it as ritualistic as you can: that is, do the cleaning with feeling. I know of some who will bury the stones in the ground for twenty-four hours, with the intention of allowing Mother Nature to put the energy back into the crystals. Others put the stones into a glass of water and place it in the window overnight to allow the moon to shine on it. There's no 'right' or 'wrong' way, only 'your' way.

Mother's recipes
When we suffer from a simple headache, do we not just reach for the paracetamol or aspirin? We trust the drug to effect the cure but never consider what the long lasting effect that the drug may have on our bodies or minds. Before the introduction of such drugs and antibiotics, doctors used natural remedies to ease aches and pains and fight illness. There were also 'Mother's recipes', handed down from generation to generation.

One simple form of practice to cure irritating headaches was to place a piece of Rose Quartz on the forehead and sit down calmly whilst holding the Rose Quartz, and relax. I know many people who still prefer this method and for many the results are just the same as using any headache pill. This method can't harm and has no side-effects. If you get a lot of headaches it's got to be worth trying. It certainly seems that using 'alternative' therapies can definitely improve our lives. Even the simplest of therapies can help us to relax and so develop a more positive and energetic outlook on life.

Forget about any complicated theories and 'wacky' practices, a lot of therapies are easy to understand, very simple to use and can be practised safely anytime and anywhere. Apart from anything else they are often fun to try and if they work for you, I am sure that you would be pleased to pass on any new-found cures to your family and friends. The wackiest that I have done was when I built a pyramid shaped tent in the lounge because I had read it gave you energy if you slept in a pyramid. These days you'll find me just wearing one of my 'Power for Life' **Dream Maker** Gemstone Power Bracelets.

I will now reproduce a list of the more popular and easily obtainable Gemstones and Crystals along with their benefits. Why not see if you are responsive to the use of them. I have found, over the years, so many people who are able to 'tune into' the vibrations of the stones. Maybe it is simply the belief that helps, but if it works, does it matter?

It goes without saying but the following information is not authoritative but a fluid interpretation, from many sources. Although there is very little chance that any Gemstone or Crystal could in fact cause any undesired reaction, readers with problems are advised to consult with their own Health Practitioner before embarking on using Gemstones as an alternative treatment, or any other method of alternative medicine.

Gemstone and Crystals' associated benefits

RED JASPER … a powerful healing stone which can help those suffering from emotional problems by balancing physical and emotional needs. Its power to give strength and console such sufferers is well known. Good for … liver, kidney, bladder problems and can improve the sense of smell.

ROSE QUARTZ … healing qualities for the mind, can help with migraine and headaches. It excites the imagination and helps to relieve pent up emotions. Lifts spirits and dispels negative thoughts. Eases both emotional and sexual imbalances and helps increase fertility. Good for … the spleen, kidneys and the circulatory system. When coupled with Hematite it can work wonders on aches and pains throughout the whole of the body.

BLACK ONYX … it can give a sense of courage and helps to discover truth. Instils calm and serenity, diminishes depression. Gives us self-control whilst aiding detachment and inspiring serenity. Good for … bone marrow and relief of stress. A protective stone worn in times of conflict, a student's friend as it encourages concentration and protects against unwise decisions.

MOTHER OF PEARL … Aptly dubbed 'The Sea of Tranquillity'. Creates physical harmony of a gentle but persuasive kind. Calms the nerves. Indicates treasure, chastity, sensitivity and strength. Good for … calcified joints and the digestive system. Relaxes and soothes the emotions. Helps with sensitivity, carries the gentle peaceful healing energy of the sea.

MOONSTONE ... Gives inspiration and enhances the emotions. Able to balance emotions and a solid friend which inspires wisdom. In India the Moonstone is a sacred gem and thought to be lucky if given by the groom to his bride. Good for ... period pains and kindred disorders, fertility and child bearing.

TIGER EYE ... inspires brave but sensible behaviour with great insight and clearer perception. The confidence stone – fights hypochondria and psychosomatic diseases. Good for ... bladder, liver, kidney, invigorates and energises.

CARNELIAN ... the friendly one, is a very highly evolved healer. A good balancer, can connect with your inner self. Good for concentration, brings joy, sociability and warmth. Good for ... rheumatism, depression, neuralgia and helps to regularise menstrual cycle.

CARNELIAN / AMETHYST ... Carnelian when coupled with Amethyst purifies the consciousness, reverses negative thoughts and develops higher mental awareness. Good for ... shaking off sluggishness and becoming vigorous and alert.

GREEN AVENTURINE ... Stabilising through inspiring independence, well-being and health. Acts as a general tonic on the physical level. A stone to encourage a higher level of meditation. Favoured by Carl Faberge, the Russian craftsman famous for 'Faberge Eggs'. A talisman, which brings good fortune. Good for ... skin conditions, losing anxiety and fears.

RHODONITE ... improves memory, calms the mind and reduces stress. Gives confidence and self-esteem. Cheers the depressed, preserves youth and retards the aging process. Helps to bring back the life force into the sick. Carries the power to unobstructed love. A special stone from Australia. Good for ... emotional trauma, mental breakdown, and spleen, kidneys, heart and blood circulation.

SODALITE … Calms and clears the mind, enhancing communication and insight with the higher self. Brings joy and relieves a heavy heart. When placed at the side of the bed it can make a sad person wake up full of the joys of spring. Imparts youth and freshness to its wearer. Good for … giving fresh energy. When combined with Rhodonite it can produce the 'Elixir of Life'.

OBSIDIAN SNOWFLAKE … For all those it recognises, a powerful healer. Keeps energy well grounded, clears subconscious blocks and brings an insight and understanding of silence, detachment, wisdom and love. A lucky Talisman, brings good fortune. Favoured by ancient Mexican cultures to neutralise negative magic. Good for … eyesight, stomach and intestines.

BLUE AGATE … Improves the ego, a supercharger of energy. A stone of strength and courage. Aids concentration. Helps to soothe all kinds of hostile feelings and allows joy into your life. Inspires serenity. Good for … stress, certain ear disorders.

AMETHYST … Aids creative thinking. Relieves insomnia when placed under the pillow. A very special and powerful aid to spiritual awareness, and healing. Very helpful for meditation, inspiration, intuition and divine love. When worn with Carnelian it will calm the overactive. A love and romance stone. Good for … Blood pressure, fits, grief and insomnia.

HEMATITE … A stone that you either like or dislike. To those who like it, it can be a very optimistic inspirer of courage and personal magnetism. Lifts gloominess and depression. When used in conjunction with Carnelian it can prevent fatigue. This stone is particular effective during pregnancy. Good for … blood, spleen and to generally strengthen the body.

ROCK CRYSTAL … This stone holds a place of unique importance in the world of gems. It enlarges the aura of everything near to it and acts as a catalyst to increase the healing powers of other minerals. Its vibrations resonate with triple-time waltz-like beat of life, giving a co-ordinating role in all holistic practices. Good for brain, soul; dispeller of negativity.

During my research, I was given the opportunity to read a book that had been printed in 1652. This book was so old that the pages had to be opened very carefully so as not to damage either the fragile paper or its outer leather cover.

The book turned out to be fascinating. I had the chance to read the original 'Old English Text' about the Magical, Mysterious, and Healing properties of Gems and Crystals.

A LAPIDARY or THE HISTORY OF
PRETIOUS STONES

With cautions for the undeceiving of all those
that deal with Pretious Stones.

Thomas Nicols

Sometimes of Jesus College in Cambridge

Printed by Thomas Buck. Printer to the Universitie
1652

Thomas Nicols was a learned man, a scholar and a translator; but couldn't understand how his fellow scholars could believe that various precious stones had supernatural mystical powers, so they explained to him their views of stories of stones changing colour for their owners as a way of showing that danger was near. The Loadstone (see extract) being magnetic had strange invisible effects on iron fillings; we know them to day as magnets and compasses.

However Thomas Nicols being a committed Christian saw these stories in very simple terms of Black or White. That is, to him, it was either God's work and therefore it was OK, being 'Divine' or it was the devil's work and therefore satanic and diabolic and to be avoided.

So it was in 1652 at Jesus College, Cambridge that Thomas Nicols produced his book on Lapidary, a guide to Gemstones and their mysterious powers.

It was only 200 years earlier that the first printing press had been produced and 100 years since Copernicus had published his treatise: that the sun is a star and that all the planets revolved around it and the earth is simply one of them. Isaac Newton was only 10 years of age and would 35 years later, from the same College, publish his theory of 'Universal Gravitation'.

So it was a credit to Thomas Nicols that he reported so faithfully the thinking of his time whilst still having so many personal doubts of his own. Nearly 350 years later, modern man can now explain many things that earlier man could not. Thomas Nicols did not know for example about the 'Placebo effect' or the 'Power of Suggestion'; the electrical field found within man or the vibrating frequency within the Crystals, or even the Earth's Magnetic Field. If he had known, then he would not have been so troubled about what his fellow scholars were saying.

Enjoy reading the following original extracts from his book, now faithfully reproduced unabridged.

Extracts from his book

"Surely, we live not in the most unknowing times of the World, nay, never was this part of the World fuller knowledge than now, it is wherein many are blest with excellent gifts and endowments by which they are enabled to enquire more thoroughly into its natures and causes of things".

Thomas Nicols 1652

Diamond ... "If a true Diamond be put upon the head of a woman without her knowledge, it will make her in her sleep if she be faithful to her husband, to cast herself into his embraces, but if she be an adulteress, to turn away from him".

Ruby ... "Worn as an amulet, or drunk, it is good against poison, and against the plague and drive away sadness".

Amethyst … "Aristotle saith of it, that it being applied to the navell, or worn about the navell, it will hinder the ascension of vapours; the reason, it draweth the vapours to its self and doth disguise them. It sharpeneth the wit, diminisheth sleep. Good for resisting of Poyson".

Saphire … "If it be worn by an adulterer, by loosing its splendour it will discover his adultery and that the wearing of it, both hinder the erections that are caused by Venus. Lustful thoughts or wicked spirit are the causes of such undue erections of the flesh … keepeth men chaste and therefore is worn of Priests".

Starre-stone "is excellent good against the plague, and to expel worms out of the body".

Malachite … "It is said to protect children from perillous and hurtful chance, and cureth them of their familiar desease, namely convultions. Superstitious persons do engrave upon it the figure of the sunne, to preserve them from incantations, and wicked spirits and venomous creatures".

Coral … "Adviseth to give to new born children as soon as they are come into the World, before they have tasted anything. Ten grains of the powder of coral in the mother's milk; which means he saith they shall be preserved all the days of their life from epilepsie".

The Gagate or Stone Coal … "a black stone of a polisht splendour generated of an oyly substance, which floweth forh the rock called Petroleum. Which being put to the fire burneth like Bitumen".

Opalus … "cloudeth the eyes of those that stand about him who wears it, so that they can either not see or not mind what is done before them; for this cause it is asserted to be a safe patron of thieves and thefts".

Topaze … "the powder of it is said to be good in Asthmatick passions, in fever to be held under the tongue it is said to quench thirst".

Agate … "strange things of the virtue of this stone as it doth excite passions, move melancholy, doth hinder the fits of the epileptic".

Cornelian … "that it causeth him that weareth it to be of a cheerful heart, free from fear and offers good protection for him against wichcrafts and fascinations".

Load-stone … "The wisdom of man which hath much searcht and enquired into the nature of this stone, hath attributed its attractive power to the planets, and to the influences of the starres, and saith that it doth receive its virtue from Lunar and Venus.

For if you cover over the Load-Stone with filings of Iron, the Load-Stone will grow more lively, as receiving a nourishment from such filings; and the residue of the filings will be changed into rust, for stones live, and have need of nourishment for their augmentation and conservation.

Cardanus saith, that Aristotle that great inquirer into nature, was altogether unknowing of the maritime use of this stone, and of that use which is made of the 'sea card' by vertue of this stone; and that Galen and Alexander Aphrodisius, two great inquirers into the secrets of nature, have not so much as once made mention of the wonderful nature of this stone.

The maritime use of it was also unknown to the Romanses. And that the reason saith Cardanus, that they suffered so many ship wracks. Merchants and Mariners in their passages under the line, have observed, that on this side of the line the 'card' doth always out the North; but when they are once past the Equinoctiall line, and are come nearer to the Antartick pole, they say it forsaketh the North, and pointeth out only the South.

The cause of this strange variation of the 'sea-card' in the passage under the line, is supposed to arise from a Magnetick mountain, which in whatsoever place it is, it is observed by the 'sea-card', Upon these grounds and reasons, it is to be surposed that there is another Magnetick mountan towards the Antartick pole". … End …

Isn't it amazing that a magnetised piece of steel looks exactly the same as an ordinary piece, and yet the magnetised one can lift over twelve times its own weight, whereas the ordinary steel could not even lift a feather.

Alchemy

Over the years I have been continually asked for various 'Healing Gifts' that would be suitable to give to loved ones, family and friends. So the idea of 'Themed' Power Gems was born. It's curious how a business can grow; but once the idea was accepted it was then that the next idea came, and that was, 'Why not use combinations of stones' and then the various titles just seemed to arrive. Using the knowledge gained after all the research, I came up with the 'Power Gem' range of gifts.

With titles such as:- 'To Remove Aches and Pains', 'The Healer', 'Fertility', 'Good Luck', 'Peace of Mind', 'For willpower', 'Imagine', 'Energy Booster', 'To Lift Depression', 'Elixir of Life', and 'Adults Only', you get the idea.

With this range my audiences could decide for themselves which 'Power Gem' would suit them most. Very quickly I discovered just how popular these were and surprisingly just how effective they were. People were not just buying them for themselves but for their family and friends. It was then that I decide to help further by writing a Mini-Guide to accompany each gift and as people wanted to know more, that was when I decided to go into writing books. Before I reproduce this Mini-Guide for you to read, I would like to relate some very interesting, and yet typical, stories.

I was giving a talk and demonstration at a local home for the elderly, a sheltered home. When I had finished, the warden, a woman in her mid-thirties, asked if I could make her a special gift for her mother, whose birthday was just a week away. She had had an idea for a gift, something a little unusual and special.

She asked me if it would be possible, by using my knowledge, to produce a Gift which would be suitable, with the title of 'Peace of Mind'. It was because every year when she had asked her mum what she would like for her birthday her mum always replied "Just give me Peace of Mind, that's all I ask, just give me 'Peace of Mind'" and that year, she did. By using Green Aventurine, Rose Quartz and Rhodonite, I was able to present the warden with her new gift, one which is now a firm favourite.

A week later I was giving a talk at a Catholic Church in Bradford (UK), where I told them this little story. Not surprisingly on that night I completely sold out and even finished up having to take orders.

One of the many testimonials received:
Dear Robert, thank you for the research that you have done to produce a great little book (Astrology the Secret Code) which has helped to settle many arguments. I am a religious education teacher in a Catholic school, a practising Catholic with a degree in history and philosophy. I have been made to feel guilty about my interest in Astrology and crystals because of my faith, but you have given me some fantastic tools to argue my corner.
Mary

At another sheltered home in Oldham (UK), many of the ladies were buying the 'Adults Only', I think as a joke. One told me that it was for her daughter as a little wedding gift, it was only for a bit of fun, and she knew that her daughter would find it amusing.

One of the care workers at the home asked if I did 'party plan', because she thought a lot of her friends and neighbours would be interested if she could hold a Party. So we made a firm date and then duly turned up on the night. One of the ladies from the sheltered home was there and she was continually warning her friends to be careful of the 'Adults Only' because, she said, "they don't half work". Only modesty stopped me from asking exactly what she meant; she looked the sort that would have told me. Because of her testament that night, you won't be surprised but I completely sold out.

Now you can read this mini book for yourselves

Power Gems

These are a unique group of Gemstones and Crystals that have been carefully linked in harmony to unite their individual mystic powers and provide a Holistic Force which can help revive Health, increase Wealth, bring Peace and provide Energy.

The concept of being treated by a lump of rock may sound odd and hard to imagine, but ancient civilisations have been doing just that since the beginning of time.

It's true that traditions, myths and supernatural stories have always been associated with the magical mysteries of Crystals, Minerals and Gemstones. For thousands of years, people have told extraordinary stories about the power that has come from within these stones.

The Sumerians and Babylonians, then the Egyptians and Greeks and even our own English ancestors not only believed in these healing properties but actually used Crystals and Gemstones for treating a wide range of ailments and conditions in everyday life.

Although these ancient beliefs may have been lost or rebuffed for the last few hundred years, some of these legends are now proven to be closer to the truth than we may have realised. Remarkable stories of complete recoveries after years of pain and misery are now becoming commonplace.

If just one Crystal or Gemstone does possess such power and does have such a potency, then just imagine how exciting the prospect of having three Crystals and Gemstones linked together. The thought of such power from each stone being united with the powers of the others and amplified can be awesome. Most Rosewood Power Gems contain three Gemstones or Crystals, a powerful number in itself, being representative of Mother Earth as well as the Holy Trinity.

The Healer ...
We have united the three most powerful Healing Gemstones and Crystals.
Carnelian ... The friendly one. It is a very evolved healer, mentioned many times in both the Old and New Testaments of the Bible.

Red Jasper ... Well known as a powerful healing stone and a provider of strength. Mentioned in the New Testament in Revelations 21:19 – "The first foundations of the walls of the New Jerusalem were made of Jasper". Represents, Aries in Astrology, the first energy of the life cycle – "On the first day of Spring, a commencement force of purest energy revitalizes the Earth".

Rock Crystal ... This stone holds a place of unique importance in the world of Gems. It enlarges the aura of everything near to it and acts as a catalyst to increase the healing powers of other minerals. Co-ordinates all holistic practices.
Power Phase :- Healing

Good Luck
These three powerful Gemstones are known for their Good Fortune.
Obsidian Snowflake ... Favoured by Ancient Mexican cultures, to neutralise negative magic. A very lucky talisman, a bringer of good fortune.
Green Aventurine ... Green is a colour associated with God and in Astrology linked with Libra. Libra is the cardinal Air sign of the Zodiac and Air is the Breath of Life. Libra is also the seventh sign of the Zodiac, which is also favoured as God's Number. Green Aventurine was favoured by Carl Faberge, the Russian craftsman famous for 'Faberge Eggs'.
Moonstone ... In India, Moonstone is a sacred gemstone and is given to the bride by the groom on their wedding day, as a token of Good Luck and Fortune. The moon has the most influence and power of all the heavenly bodies over our Earth.
Power Phrase :- My Luck's returned, I give thanks

Peace of Mind
A combination of stones to bring peace, harmony and tranquillity into your surroundings; to capture stillness in movement.
Green Aventurine ... Green is said to be God's colour. A stone well known for easing anxiety and fears. A talisman, a bringer of good fortune.
Rose Quartz ... A love stone, which also helps to relieve migraine and headaches. Releases pent up emotions, high spirits and dispels negative thoughts.
Rhodonite ... Improves memory, calms the mind, reduces stress, gives confidence and self-esteem. Cheers the depressed, preserves youth and retards the ageing process, a very special stone.
Power Phase :- Relax

For Willpower

The most powerful combination of stone and crystal which can be used to boost our willpower e.g. to lose weight or stop smoking.

Rose Quartz ... Healing qualities for the mind, helps to release pent up emotions whilst dispelling negative thoughts.

Black Onyx ... It can give a sense of courage and helps to discover truth. Gives self-control, whilst aiding detachment. Helps relieve stress.

Rock Crystal ... This stone holds a place of unique importance in the world of gems. It enlarges the aura of everything near to it and acts as a catalyst to increase the healing powers of other minerals. Co-ordinates all holistic practices.

Power Phrase:- I can and I will.

Adults Only

These powerful stones combine to create the most imaginative aphrodisiac. A very sensuous combination.

Rose Quartz ... Well known as a love stone with a beautiful colour of pink.

Amethyst ... A romantic stone, very helpful for meditation, inspiration and divine love.

Carnelian ... A stone on the breastplate of King Solomon. This power stone represents passion and energy and like Amethyst, Carnelian contains iron traces which give it its seductive colour. A solid dependable stone.

Power Phrase:- Bring my lover to me.

To Remove Aches and Pains

Three Gemstones designed for easing aches and pains.

Rose Quartz ... Rose Quartz is made up of minute crystals with traces of Titanium, a metallic element, which gives it profound strength.

Hematite ... There are many ailments which benefit from a source of iron. When united with Rose Quartz, this steel-like stone works wonders with aching bones and bruised skin.

Rock Crystal ... Once again the Rock Crystal acts as a catalyst to increase the active powers within Rose Quartz and Hematite.

Power Phrase:- Healing light shine on me.

To Lift Depression

Three powerful Gemstones, which bring joy and happiness and remove sadness.
Carnelian ... The friendly one. Carnelian is a highly evolved healing stone. Providing good concentration. Brings joy, sociability and warmth.
Hematite ... To those who like it, it can be a very optimistic inspirer of courage and personal magnetism. Lifts gloominess and depression.
Tiger Eye ... Inspires brave, sensible behaviour. The confidence stone, fights hypochondria and psychosomatic diseases.
Power Phrase:- From sorrow to joy.

Elixir of Life

To produce an Elixir, we should first wash the Gemstones. Then place them in a glass of clear water and leave them overnight, ideally in the light of a full moon. The Elixir of Life should be sipped slowly in a ritualistic manner. This is a powerful approach, which appeals ideally to the imagination.
Rhodonite ... Preserves youth and retards the ageing process. Helps to bring back the life force in to the sick, carries the power to the unobstructed love. A very special stone.
Sodalite ... Brings joy and relieves a heavy heart. Imparts youth and freshness to its wearer. (When combined with Rhodonite, can produce the Elixir of Life).
Power Phrase:- Life force grow in me.

Energy Booster

A combination of three gemstones to boost energy.
Carnelian ... Good for shaking off sluggishness and helps us become more vigorous and alert. A gemstone used on the breastplate of King Solomon, maybe to boost his energy, perhaps because he was known to have had 1,000 wives. Carnelian is associated with Virgo, the sixth sign of the Zodiac and the element Earth.
Amethyst ... When coupled with Carnelian, Amethyst becomes a very powerful energy booster. Amethyst is tinted by irradiated iron and iron is one of the six active body minerals essential for life. It strengthens muscles, enriches the blood and increases resistance to illness.
Rock Crystal ... Has the power to enlarge the aura of other Gemstones and in this case it increases power to store energy. In Greek mythology, Rock Crystal was known as Holy Water frozen by the Gods of Olympus.
Power Phrase:- Energised Vitality

Imagine

We use the lovely title from John Lennon's song "Imagine", as these stones really are designed for a very special purpose. Power beyond imagination holds the key to all changes of life. The fine tints of these stones are designed to help us reach a level within the mind, where all things become possible.

Rose Quartz ... Helps to excite the imagination, helps to relieve pent up emotion. Lifts spirits and dispels negative thoughts.

Amethyst ... Aids creative thinking. A very special and powerful aid to spiritual awareness. Very helpful for meditation inspiration and intuition.

Green Aventurine ... Green is said to be God's colour. Stabilising through inspiring independence. A stone to encourage a higher level of meditation.

Power Phase:- Imagination

A Power beyond imagination?

Many scholars and philosophers have stated that man is master of his own destiny.

Man has fully mastered his environment planet earth, the land, the seas and the skies. He can travel around his world at will. He has built bridges, dug tunnels, he can travel both under and over water. He can fly higher and faster than any bird, he's travelled millions of miles into space and successfully travelled to the moon and back.

So what makes man so special? He has learned to use the power of imagination from deep inside the subconscious part of his mind, to conquer his environment and create the machinery to conquer the whole planet.

To have knowledge of the powers within the subconscious mind leads straight to the super highway of the mind, this then brings forth all kinds of riches including spiritual, mental, physical as well as financial.

Understand that energy, translated into thoughts, emotions and feelings, is the cause of all our experience and so the cause of all effects. With this thought in mind, we should learn how to use this subconscious power.

Power that can heal the sick, lift fear and depression and free us from the restrictions of poverty, want and misery. It can break the chains of repression for ever.

What we have to do is be quite clear of the needs we wish to embody, and the creative powers of our subconscious mind will respond accordingly. Draw deep upon the 'Power beyond Imagination' and you will uncover a completely new experience of life.

The Bible says in a simple, clear and beautiful way:- "Whosoever shall say unto this mountain, be thou removed, and be thou cast into this sea, and shall not doubt in his heart, but shall believe that those things which he saith shall come to pass, he shall have whatsoever he saith".

How I moved a mountain

Have you ever won the lottery? I am often asked. Not yet, I reply; however I did move a mountain, does that count?

Using the very same techniques you are reading about I was able to move a mountain.

It all really started in a small boarding house in South Wales. I was there on a business trip and it was early evening when one of the guests gave me a book. It turned out to be not just any book, but Napoleon Hill's classic 'Think and Grow Rich'. It's a very inspirational book and I can highly recommend it. It certainly captured my imagination, and it gave me the insight, and the tools on how to use my imagination, and the results were simply staggering. No wonder Albert Einstein said "Imagination is more important than knowledge". For example:-

My father owned a joiner's workshop in a typical Yorkshire village. Most of the housing, being terraced, had been built to provide accommodation for the local mill's workforce. All the houses were built using stone from the local quarry; this quarry provided all the 'Yorkshire Stone' that was needed to build not only the houses but the mills as well.

At the rear of my father's workshop was a huge hillside, it was so steep it was almost vertical. It was man made from the 'tipping', over many years, of the quarry waste. The quarry had been disused for many years and of no interest to anybody, and it had no real value because it was land locked. However I had an idea and so I bought it. I thought if I could move it, the mountain that is, then my idea was to build houses on it.

There was an advertising feature article in the local paper about me; here are just some of the extracts.

It must have called for faith that moves mountains to even consider starting such a project. Faith and JCBs and giant diggers .....

Robert Wood, who conceived the idea initially, claims that he was helped by not knowing enough to be fully aware of the difficulties to be overcome. Experts were horrified. One of the planners inspecting the site remarked that he was almost tempted to recommend planning permission just to see if it could be done.

.... Words and pictures can give little idea of the unique magnificence of the site. Not quite up to the Grand Canyon, but breath-taking in its audacity.

I even had a mention in a Local History book with a picture of my new house and a caption:- *Executive housing for the 21st century.*

Mark 11 : 23
> *Therefore I tell you, whatever you ask for in prayer,*
> *believe that you have received it, and it will be yours.*

Later, however on learning how to use our natural 'Inner power', we can open the prison doors of fear and enter into a life described by Paul as the glorious liberty of the sons of God.

Three magic steps

First find a quiet peaceful place to relax, start by just being aware of your breathing, just relax, and then secondly, concentrate on a short phrase, a power phrase. One that can easily be remembered; it's a little like a lullaby or mantra. This can be done within the quiet of the mind or if you prefer spoken out load. Either way will help it to enter into your subconscious mind. Repeat this two or three times a day for a few minutes at a time.

Finally, as you are going to sleep each night, practise repeating your power phrase – for example 'health' – quietly, easily and with feeling. Do this over and over again, just like a lullaby. Lull yourself to sleep with the word 'health' firmly fixed in your mind. You will soon be aware of changes, changes that will be for the 'good'. Now here is a 'key': you must, and this isn't easy, on awaking repeat your mantra, your lullaby. This is important: you must, first thing, lightly touch your chosen Gemstone or stones.

Once you can instinctively touch your stones and repeat your power phrase on waking you will have arrived at a level of mind that will bring about all the changes you have desired. The phrase 'health' can be substituted for any one of the other phrases or any you may have found for yourself. What we are trying to do here is to excite the imagination, and repetition is one way, but there are other ways. It's finding the best way for you.

One of the simplest ways to benefit from crystal power is to wear one or carry them with you, and at night have them close whilst sleeping.

During my many talks and displays, over many years, I have experimented with my audiences by passing around Rose Quartz and Hematite. Simply because my research had shown that these two stones, when coupled together are very good for helping with aches and pains. And the results of passing them around didn't disappoint. In fact the results were quite positive. I must admit I was pleasantly surprised and I still am with all the fabulous stories that I regularly hear.

I have given talks to thousands of people, over the years. It was at one such talk that someone told me they noticed just how cold the stones had gone. This was despite the fact that they were warm when they received them.

Then someone else said that the stones had become very hot, almost unbearable, and added that they could feel a kind of tingle going through their arm. Another said that they could feel heat going through their body, as though they were being warmed up from the inside, a very enjoyable feeling. Obviously there must be 'something' and this 'something' seems to affect people in different ways.

To help understand what may be happening, there is a demonstration that I do just to show the power that's held within crystals. I take two small pieces of Rose Quartz and in subdued lighting; I gently rub the two stones together. Most people are surprised to see the stones light up. It's quite a spectacular way of showing the stones' power. There is a technical name for this strange phenomenon which is the 'Piezoelectric Effect'. the production of electricity or electrical polarity by applying a mechanical stress to certain crystals. Rubbing them together causes this effect.

I then explain that most people seem to be responsive to certain crystals and it really doesn't matter whether they 'Believe' or not, the effect on them when it happens is real. I now realise that these experiences happen to someone every time at the talks. However, the experiences are not always the same; some people respond far more than others do and I never know who will be affected by the crystals.

From all this knowledge came our exciting 'Power for Life' range of books and a very interesting 'Themed' range of power Bracelets. For those who can enjoy that feeling of connection with the esoteric nature of Gemstones and Crystals, then our 'Power for Life' Power bracelets could be ideal for you. For further details why not visit my website:-
www.rosewood-gifts .co.uk

PART THREE
Revealing the 'Formula'
with facts and theories – you just can't ignore.

In the first part of this book, I wrote about Astrology and especially 'Birthstones', their attributed powers and ancient man's belief in them.

In the second part, I wrote about the 'Healing Power' of Gemstones and Crystals and the healing powers associated with each individual stone.

I have taken the view not to judge these qualities but to present them in as honest and non-judgmental a fashion as I can. My view is that, although I don't fully understand how the 'Hidden Power' works, nevertheless it has to be said that, for many, there is no doubt that the 'Hidden Power' does work through Gemstones and Crystals. I would like to now spend more time on a 'Formula' that I think can go a long way into explaining all this.

A journey of a thousand miles.

I now think it would prove useful if I could explain how I actually got involved with this fascinating subject. The old cliché of a journey of a thousand miles starts with a single step, although a cliché, is very true.

My journey started on a day in February 1986, when a series of adverts were appearing in many magazines promoting a free booklet and information guide on the 'Power for Living'.

It changed me from a property developer into a qualified hypnotherapist, and then led me to give talks and displays on the mysteries surrounding Gemstones and Crystals whilst demonstrating the healing power, using Crystals.

These days I find myself being invited to many churches. My talk is Christian-based but not intended to be religious. I speak the Church's language but change it especially for those who wouldn't dream of going to a church.

For example, if you take what the Church says about 'the power of prayer', and change the expression to 'the power of thought', then the power is no longer exclusive to the Church but is where it should be, back to its roots, within each and every one of us. "Discover the kingdom within, because the Kingdom of God is within you" (Luke 17:21)

You will understand why I do what I do. It's because of instructions, a feeling, and an intuition that seemed to be coming to me through my mind. De-mystify the Mysteries and tell people, "Why try to predict the future when you are the ones who can change it? That's why you have *free will*". These thoughts I have found, over the years, to be all-consuming. And over the years I have slowly been given an 'understanding'.

So I haven't been able to do anything other than try and act upon these deeply-hidden instructions that only I was aware of, and within these writings I expect to fulfil these instructions to the best of my ability.

Power for Living – Chapter 1

In February 1986 I sent away for a booklet entitled 'Power for Living'. I was, and had been for many years; involved with sales and marketing, and thought anything that might give me an edge must be worth looking into. Besides, it was FREE, so I had nothing to lose – except, as it turned out, my ignorance.

The package duly arrived, and I opened it – only to discover it wasn't what I had thought. Maybe I should have known because (though I haven't mentioned this) it was being promoted with a picture of Cliff Richard and Gerry Williams, a well-known BBC commentator.

It turned out to be more of a religious type of booklet. "What a con," I thought; I would not have sent for it, had I known. So why I didn't throw it in the bin, I don't know. Instead I put it in the car, thinking that next time I was bored at least I would have something to look at.

It wasn't long before I did have the time and started to read it – which didn't take long. The Gospel of St. John was paraphrased, and the concluding section began with a prayer: "Lord, I thank you for paying for the sins I have committed. I give my life to you. Teach me the right way to live". Amen. "If you have believed in Christ now for the first time write your name and today's date on the blank lines as a record of the time of your salvation."

And I did.

Robert W. Wood
Feb. 1986.

I remember thinking, "And why not! If there is anybody out there … then show me".

I Knew it …

Nothing.

Whilst I was waiting, I carried on reading and realised that my part of the bargain, or so it seemed, was to read the prayer, and this, it said, would allow Jesus to enter my life by invitation. I was to complete this invitation by signing it and dating it, and this I had done.

I thought, OK, if you can't show me there's somebody there, why not give me an example by showing me, say, a door opening when there's nobody there. That'll do it, I thought.

Maybe it was only in my mind, but to my amazement the door seemed to move. I nearly fell off my chair. However, within the next three days I knew beyond a shadow of a doubt that something had happened – but I didn't have a clue what!

I remember saying to Moira, my wife, "I have this strange, unusual feeling that I should go to church." But which church?

Let me explain: I had never been to church except for a few weddings, including my own. I was so nervous on my wedding day that although at the time I smoked (I was only nineteen) I was too nervous to have a cigarette. All my three children were christened not because of me, but because Moira wanted them to be.

I remember, only too well, one time when the vicar arrived at our house, presumably to discuss a christening. He arrived in his car at exactly the same time as I was reversing my car out of the drive. I didn't see him and ran straight into the side of his car, with him still in it. He was a true Christian. I don't remember him being angry or annoyed. If it had been me, on the other hand I would have coloured the air blue. Maybe he would have liked to, but it wasn't that easy for him, with wearing a 'dog collar'.

Up to the age of 38 I had never 'been to church'. I even avoided all the children's Christmas parties; I wanted nothing to do with anything remotely 'religious'.

Back to my 'feeling': Moira asked me, "Which church do you intend to go to, then?" "I don't know," was my reply. "I just feel I should. But if it's intended I will somehow know. Maybe I'll be given a sign."

A Feeling ...
From then onwards, every time we went out in the car and passed a church, I used to say out loud, "Is it this church?" But alas, I didn't seem to be getting a reply – and yet I knew I would. It would only be a matter of time. I just had a 'feeling'.

Three or four months had passed by and nothing had happened, but the 'feeling' wouldn't go away; in fact, it seemed to be getting stronger. Then one day someone I had known for years was doing a small job of signwriting for me at work, and whilst we were casually talking I discovered he was in a choir at St Steven's Church.

Now this started to feel right, because this was the church where all my children had been christened, and in fact my elder sister Jean had been married there many years earlier; but it was no longer my local church as we had moved out of the catchment area.

Although it seemed right, I then remembered this was where the vicar whom I had run into with my car had come from. My 'feeling' that this was right grew stronger and stronger. I felt this was finally the sign I had been waiting for. St Steven's was the church I would go to.

A journey into the unknown – chapter 2

Sunday had arrived. I put on my best suit; for the first time in my life, I was going to church not because I had to, but because I wanted to.

I was feeling apprehensive, and, either in support or out of curiosity, my family decided to join me – Moira and my two daughters Carolyn and Kimberley. My son Christopher gave it a miss. It felt strange. And I was nervous and excited at the same time.

However, I was not prepared for what happened that first Sunday morning. I didn't realise just how traumatic going to church can be. I will always now spare a thought for a stranger in unfamiliar surroundings. Going to church seems so ordinary, now, but the fact is that the first time it was a culture shock for both me and my family.

You see, because none of us had ever 'been to church' before, even the simplest of things seemed difficult.

Let me explain. As we walked into the church we were welcomed and given a hymn book, plus another book that said Rite A – The Alternative Service Book 1980. This seemed to be the instructions for the service, but why start at page 119? I don't mean we turned to page 119, but the first page after the introduction was page 119. And why did the vicar say that today he would be using the third Eucharistic prayer? Why not the first or the second? What on earth was he talking about? And why should we be singing 'Gloria in Excelsis' when according to my book it was to be said?

Did I hear him say something about a Peace? – I didn't realise there was a war. I might just as well have been listening to a foreign language, for all the sense it made to me.

The service started – and, looking back, it seems that a very strange thing occurred. We must have really looked out of place, and a woman who was sitting just behind us must have realised we didn't have a clue, because she kept swapping her book – which was on the right page – for mine, which wasn't. This carried on throughout the whole of the service. At the time it was just what we needed; she was being very helpful.

We sang hymns, heard readings, sometimes we stood and at other times we sat. We did something called 'Peace', where everybody just seemed to smile at everybody else – especially the woman behind us who had been so helpful. We did the offering (that's when the money is collected) but the best was yet to come.

Near the end of the service people were starting to go out to the front of the church. I quietly asked Moira if she knew where they were going. "I don't know," she replied. "Well, wherever it is I am not going," I said quite definitely, feeling nervous and anxious.

We were sitting in the middle of the church, to the left of the central aisle. I could see that someone, whom I now know to have been the church warden, was standing at the end of each pew in turn, beckoning everyone in that pew to go to the front. To my horror I saw everybody, row by row, slowly getting up and leaving to go to the front. It was starting to look very empty in front of us as each pew cleared and the warden came nearer and nearer to us.

I could see that there was something happening amongst the Choir, they seemed to be eating something and then having a drink out of a very large silver-looking cup. Oh! It was disgusting; they were all drinking from the same cup. Didn't they care that they'd get each other's germs?

Then, a miracle – I had such a feeling of utter relief when, just two rows in front of us, a couple declined to go up. Thank God, we wouldn't be the only ones if we didn't go; and we didn't. What I didn't know was that they were taking Communion.

The vicar concluded the service by saying, "Go in Peace to love and serve the Lord. Amen," and then slowly walked out with the choir behind him. I shot out of that church, grateful to have survived.

Not at all what I had expected.

I was 38 years of age. I felt like a child who was shocked, traumatised – a feeling I shall never forget. And yet all I had done was attend a regular Church of England Sunday service!

The question was asked, "Will you go back again, Dad?" My answer was, "YES! I shall, but I don't expect anyone else to."

It's strange, looking back; but all the fear, trauma and anxiety of going to church for the first time was not as great as the overwhelming 'feeling' that I had to.

I went on to spend some time at that church, even becoming a sidesman, and I never missed a service for at least two years. I noticed that the lady who had really helped to sort us out that first time never sat in that place again. She was one of the church lay readers and always seemed to sit on the right of the centre aisle, and always near the front.

I don't think anyone who is used to going to church could understand the amount of effort it takes to go for the first time. Most people go with someone else who can show them the ropes. I didn't; I hadn't even been to Sunday school; I had no indoctrination of any kind into religion. I was a blank sheet of paper, waiting to be filled. Looking back now, I realised with sadness that I never went to my children's Christmas services because I wouldn't have anything to do with something I didn't understand.

The following week I went to church again with Moira; the girls stayed at home. The second visit was much more relaxed. I now had a fair idea what to expect. It turned out that the people were going out to the front to take part in the Eucharist, or Communion – "the Christian sacrament in which Christ's Last Supper is commemorated by the consecration of bread and wine." I noticed there were a lot more people who didn't go out, so I didn't feel conscious of standing out any more. We always seemed to sit near the back of the church, always to the left of the central aisle. Isn't it strange – although you could sit anywhere you wished, we nearly always sat in the same place, as did most other people.

As we were leaving the church, the vicar seemed to notice us – maybe a vicar should. It was a look which only lasted a moment, but I saw it. I realised I had been noticed when a few weeks later Michael, the vicar, turned up at my door. To this day I don't think he ever said why he called, he just kept coming. In a way I loved it. I was curious. I had a thousand questions I wanted to ask. Without saying anything, he seemed to understand that something was happening to me – even though I didn't understand it myself.

I kept going to church each week, and Michael kept visiting. The conversation came around to me being confirmed – how did I feel about this? The feelings of that first visit came back to mind; this would be quite a commitment. This time, my 'feeling' that I should was getting stronger and stronger. It reminded me of being invited to act in a play – but first I had to learn my lines. So it was like being in the wings, waiting for my turn; I was watching, listening, learning, and saying nothing, only because I had nothing to say.

A date was fixed, and I and fifteen others were confirmed by the Bishop of Wakefield, Bishop David Hope. This was February 1987, just one year to the day that I had signed my prayer and dated it.

Once confirmed, I didn't know what to expect. It seemed more like an anti-climax. Although I felt I was ready, willing and able, nothing seemed to be happening. So I just got on with my life.

Two years later I had still not read the Bible. I had read, instead, many books about the Bible – but not the Bible Itself.

I was invited to a friend's daughter's confirmation, which was at the same church where Moira and I got married on Saturday 31st August 1968.

I can't remember how I came to have it – whether someone else had bought it, or whether I had – but I was wearing a small brooch in the shape of a fish, for the first time that day (14th March 1989). There are times in everybody's life when things happen that can change the direction of life for ever. What happened to me next was that kind of event.

The service had finished and the vicar had announced that coffee would be served at the back of the church.

We had not intended to stay for coffee. The church was really full, with Moira and I sitting on the left hand side of the church, a third of the way down from the back. Moira said "Let's go, we don't really know anybody so let's go." But I had a 'feeling'. "No", I said, "wait a moment." Again Moira said, "Let's go," and started to get up. But I repeated, "Wait," and for some reason unknown to me I was getting annoyed with her for wanting to leave. "Wait," I said again, "something's going to happen. "My 'feeling', or intuition, told me that I had to wait.

So we sat there while the church slowly emptied. Then I said, "It's OK, we can go now," It was as if by magic; as if I was being directed, not by a voice but by a 'feeling'.

Moira just thought I was mad.

We edged our way to the centre aisle, which was very busy, and as I was making my way to the back of the church and the way out, someone seemed to jump out in front of me saying. "Ah! I see another committed Christian."

I looked round to see who he was talking about – but what I hadn't realised was that he had seen my brooch, in the sign of the fish, the one I was wearing for the very first time that day. I had always been a little scared to wear it in case somebody asked me about it. I had already had a few 'run-ins' with friends who knew I'd 'caught religion'.

This man introduced himself as Clinton, and told me he was starting a Christians in Business luncheon group, and that the very first meeting would be the following Wednesday. Rooms had been booked in a local hotel, and he would like to invite me to come.

Clinton owns a very large wholesale business supplying Gemstones, fossils and minerals as well as jewellery components to the trade – a very successful business, by any standards. I had never met him before, but my business partner had, and I think this is how he knew that I might be interested. And although I didn't realise it at the time, during the recession of the 1980s, my business started to decline. I spent a lot of time with Clinton and for the next few years we both continued to grow within our Christian faith.

The luncheon meetings were helping me to grow within my Christian faith, and my 'feeling' was getting stronger. However, talking to some of the others made me realise my own ignorance of the scriptures. I had to admit I still hadn't read any of the Bible. So I started attending a Bible Study Group at Clinton's house. I also listened to guest speakers at various religious groups. By this time I was a sidesman at St Stevens, the church where I had been confirmed, but I was now ready for more. The 'feeling' was still growing.

I enjoyed the Wednesday luncheon group so much that I decide it was time for me to move on, and I changed churches. I tried Clinton's church, still Church of England but more charismatic, very active, and with a buzz that I enjoyed.

I recall one day the sermon included asking everyone to pray for a group of students who were said to be practising the occult.

The local minister was apparently quite concerned that they were, for fun, doing tarot reading and playing on an Ouija board.

Now, this is a board on which are marked the letters of the alphabet. Answers to questions are spelled out by a pointer or glass and are supposedly formed by spirits. I have a different explanation; but for now let me just say that the Church takes a very dim view of this type of activity, and I must say my own view is that it's not to be recommended, though not for the same reasons as those put forward by the Church (more about this later). I will just add that one of the questions that may be asked of anybody seeking to visit a hypnotherapist is, "Have you ever played with an Ouija board?" The consequences could be quite disconcerting.

I remember thinking, "There's no chance of these people coming to church, we ought to be able to go to them, but in order to communicate with them we would have to change our language."

Maybe it is this thought that has stuck with me.

As my business declined, I became interested in a total change of career and was attracted by the following advert that had appeared in my Sunday paper:

'Home study or In-House
Train in Analytical Hypnotherapy
Fascinating psychology course for an
internationally-recognised diploma
Unrivalled for self-understanding and training for private practice.'

A complete change of direction …

So I started the course, and then qualified in 1992.

There have been many occasions after my talks when someone would say, "Really it's all in the mind isn't it?" Now it's here that I have to become judgmental, because I believe that this statement or question could be true.

I believe that each and every one of us, irrespective of colour, creed or religion, is empowered with energy, a power that is so awesome, when triggered, it can heal, it can change your luck, and it can even 'move mountains'. It can give 'Life changing' experiences.

So it's us, and not the stones?

Not quite!

The stones and crystals seem to act as 'catalyst', just as the 'Placebo Effect' has to have its sugar coated pill. The stones are the triggers that help to create the desired effect.

Imagine for example two common products, bread and wine. Then add the words Communion or Eucharist and these two common every day products begin to take on a different meaning, they now become, within the mind, something else entirely.

Here's a thought: what if it's the healer that's doing the work and not the crystal? Would it matter, as long as the effect we required was working? As long as we were benefiting from the experience, does it really matter how?

I believe it does! If you had a secret benefactor wouldn't you like to know who he or she was and why?

It's true that a belief in any form of treatment will help, of that I have no doubt, remember the placebo effect.

'An inactive substance that is administered to a patient who will benefit by the psychological deception, and is mainly given with the intention of bringing about a positive therapeutic effect'.

However, where does this power of 'belief' begin, where can we find it and more importantly how can we use it constructively, intelligently for the benefit of ourselves and others? Is the answer: 'It's in the Mind'?

I have given up counting the number of times that people have said to me, "It's all in the mind". Some will even say it, almost in a dismissive way. "Oh, it's only in the mind". Try telling people who suffer from depression or those suffering from ulcers brought about by stress and worry, 'it's only in the mind'. Although the statement in itself may be true, it really doesn't tell us anything, does it?

Maybe it is all in the Mind but it would be remiss of me if I said it was, and then didn't follow with an explanation as to what I meant.

It may help if I clarify what I hope you will find within the pages of this book. I will present an explanation that I believe will go much further in explaining the meanings behind these three common statements.
1. You have to believe in it.
2. It's all in the mind.
3. It's mind over matter.

During my talks, I tell my audiences that you do not have to believe, for Crystal Healing to work. If the stones can do what they say they can do, then let them, and it's up to you to be the judge of it. If they have worked for you, then there's no doubt you would believe.

Now let's take 'it's all in the mind' as representing all three statements. Let's assume this statement to be true. We have to start somewhere and here is as good a place as anywhere. If we continue to make assumptions, that it is true, then somewhere there must be a hidden code, so let's start by becoming code breakers. Let's explore the workings within the mind.

For example if you are involved in an emergency situation and are in the United Kingdom, it would be very useful if you knew that the telephone dialling code for help is 999. In America it would be 911 and the European Union 112.

If you knew this, then help could be quickly summoned. So I think you must agree, it would be well worth your while if you knew these codes well in advance of being involved in any emergency.

I am reminded of when I went to the Library in Leeds. I was seeking addresses for my mailing lists to send to prospective groups. At most Libraries you could sit down and just wade through their files make notes and even take photocopies. Not at Leeds though, there I was shown to a table and on this table was to me my worst nightmare, the dreaded computer.

I dreaded it because I had managed to get to fifty years of age without ever having had to use a computer keyboard. I know this will sound ridiculous today but we are talking about a time when computers were quite rare and bulky, well before home computers. However here I was suddenly being confronted by the prospect of having to use it when I didn't have a clue how to use it.

Yes, I understood that it contained all the information I needed and all I had to do was to access it. At that time a computer made as much sense as those people who say 'it's all in the mind'. I knew the information was in the computer's memory, but how did you get it out, how do I get it to work?

I didn't have long to wait, the librarian could see I was having difficulties and took pity on me. She showed me how to turn it on and then pressed a few more buttons and then said "There you are all ready, just press this and that and the information will come up on the screen".

After years of self-doubt, it sounded so simple. It was easy, until I pressed a key that deleted the whole programme and I found myself back at square one, once again looking dismally at a blank screen.

The next time the assistant came to help, I made a few notes and within just a few moments I had all the information that I could ever want.

The moral of this story is simple: it was a fact that, although the information I needed was there all the time, it took someone else to show me just how to get to it, merely because I didn't know how to access it myself.

Look at electricity as an analogy. Although we know that our electricity is supplied by a local electricity board and they now in the UK act only as distributors, wouldn't it be useful if we knew that the real power was coming from a huge Power Station. It would be even better if we discovered you could go direct and secure your supply, cutting out the middleman.

There might be only one electricity, but it comes with many names and descriptions, AC or DC. It might be supplied via overhead cables or cables buried far beneath the ground.

Electricity can be generated by 'Hydro', 'wind' or even 'solar power', energy known as replenishable resources, which cause no problems to our environment or the planet. On the other hand our electricity can be generated by burning fossil fuels, coal and natural gas, but these are not renewable resources and are known to cause harm to the environment and our planet.

So although we only have the one product being produced, electricity, it would be foolish if we didn't take into account how the final product was being produced. One way has a positive effect, whilst the other has a negative effect.

Just as there is only one 'electricity'. I believe that there is only one source of 'hidden power'. So it's one thing saying 'it's all in the mind' but quite another subject altogether explaining exactly where and how it's in the mind.

Life is like a tin of Sardines,
We are all of us looking for the key.

Becoming Empowered

With the help of suggestions, explanations and information, I believe once you have grasped its meaning, and you will, it will empower you with a knowledge that will make a difference. A knowledge that will allow you to take control, and once in charge you will see life in a different way and then, 'Eureka', you will see just how crystal healing works.

Embrace a healthy scepticism, keep an open mind and let's start at the beginning. What we are about to seek cannot be seen in a normal way and yet in another way it can be seen quite clearly. Let me explain.

Cause and Effect

One very essential anchor in my life, other than my faith, is my belief in 'cause and effect'. There cannot be any effect without there being a cause. This statement of fact is set in 'Granite'. It gives a reassurance that we all need sometimes to make sense of things, when there seems to be no sense.

Just because we can't see something, it doesn't mean it's not there. For example, I cannot see the influence of the moon on the sea and yet I know it is the moon that is the cause behind the effect of the tides.

At home, I have a lovely print of an L.S. Lowry. I know that it is a Lowry because he signed the original picture but if he hadn't signed the original, I would still know it was his because of his famous match stick men and women. Although I have never met Mr Lowry, there is no doubt in my mind that he existed, because of his work, in this case a picture.

To understand precisely what we are seeking, imagine you're about to clean your house. No doubt at some time you'll want to use the vacuum cleaner. This might be any type, new or old, upright or squat, 750 watts or super turbo 2000 with all the attachments. They are all different but have one thing in common. Without exception they all need to be connected to a power source if they are to function.

Without this power source none of them could ever work. The same applies to computers, it doesn't matter how powerful or ingenious it is, whether it is ten years old or the very latest model; without being connected to a power source, they are all completely useless.

A power source worth discovering
Discovering this power source and how to connect to it is every human being's heritage, a free gift built deep into our human DNA, the very heart of our genetics. This secret ingredient, once discovered, explains the greatest mystery that surrounds Crystal Healing, why Crystal Healing Works.

Religions are very much like petrol stations,
many different brands
selling but one common product – Fuel.

Ancient wisdom suggests that the relationship between a 'Healing Crystal' and the person using it is very much individual. For over 6,000 years ancient wisdoms have always known that there is a force that although invisible, nevertheless plays a vital role in all health, holistic healing and esoteric practices. This power or force has been called by many names but for now we will simply call it the 'Universal Life Force'.

Although we are all unique and no single therapy could possibly be suitable for us all, Crystal Healing goes a long way for the majority of us. It is perfectly safe, completely non-addictive and has no side effects at all.

Thankfully, what is known as 'Esoteric', that is, Secret or Mysterious, is gradually finding acceptance amongst a new generation of Scientists and Psychologists, who realise that the human experience cannot be explained by scientific proof alone. Who would not be impressed at man's ability to land on the moon, send probes to Mars and beyond. Yet it remains a fact that if you asked a nuclear physicist how to resolve a moral dilemma, they would probably suggest you looked elsewhere for the answer. They probably couldn't help

Equally, with Crystal Healing science seems unable to help us. Of course crystal healing belongs to the category of phenomena without form, substance or colour. It is not susceptible to investigation by external means. This doesn't mean that it doesn't exist; merely that science can't explain it.

Here's a question: would you be impressed if I said, 'By using a touch of mystery, by revealing a secret 'Formula', by showing you a deeply hidden ingredient which, once revealed and understood, will change your very future'?

If I could de-mystify the mysteries and show you, beyond any doubt, how to turn your Birthstone into a special powerful Talisman and at the same time show you how to get your Healing Crystal to become so effective that you will be amazed and astounded by its power. If I told you that all this can be done by you, because you have the Power that's beyond your Imagination and then help you to discover it, and then go on to show you how to use it, would you be impressed?

Because this is exactly just what I have been doing, quietly, for many years, with the help of my talks, with stunning effect.

So, would you be impressed? Because that is exactly what this book is all about.

A Very Personal Experience
On July 15th 1991, I attended a four-day retreat; it was called the 'Inner Child Workshop' and organised by two 'Sisters' from the Cenacle. The name Cenacle refers to the room where the last supper was celebrated and the Holy Spirit descended on to the apostles. This is a small convent in Surrey, but not an enclosed or cloistered community. They are said to have a mission to influence people outside and spread the word of God. They have an international congregation, ministering to both men and women of all faiths.

I first met Sister Sue Cash, the retreat secretary at a weekend retreat held in Manchester the year before.

I don't know how or who invited her but the next time I met her was at my local Church. She had been invited to demonstrate meditational prayer techniques.

She remembered me and suggested that I might be interested in a four day long retreat in July called the 'Inner Child Workshop'. The event was advertised as a workshop to explore the connections between childhood woundedness and areas of adult life. It was run by two sisters, one I believe was well known to the Queen Mother and the other had been to a university in America as part of her studies within the church. They were both very knowledgeable.

Apparently it had already been well over subscribed but there was an acute shortage of men. "Why not apply?" she suggested, so I did and I was accepted. At the time I was studying to become a hypnotherapist and thought that this workshop could help me to understand some of my studies.

Over the years, I have been to quite a few retreats. However I was a little surprised to receive a letter pointing out that if I didn't have counselling facilities or a spiritual director, that the Cenacle couldn't take any responsibility for anything that may surface during the four day workshop. It then went on to say, 'I would urge you therefore to reflect very carefully as to whether you still wish to attend this course'.

Now this sounded serious. I did wonder what I was letting myself in for, and so I did, as a precaution, make sure that I had counselling available if it was required. As it turned out these warnings were very much justified.

This story is now going to get even stranger; as I was walking past a neighbour's house, I had one of those feelings. I was literally told, within my mind, to ask my neighbour Maurice if he would like to come along with me. I know it sounds strange but it's what really happened.

So I knocked on his door as instructed, slightly embarrassed and asked him if he would be interested in going on a four-day retreat.

I explained I seemed to have been 'instructed' to ask him and it was up to him if he was interested. I gave him the details and said he could let me know later. I must admit I didn't really think he would be all that interested; not many people would have been. Two hours later he called at my house, saying that he would like to go and could I arrange it. I must say I was genuinely very surprised and so Maurice came along as well.

The retreat
At the retreat there were 34 of us in total. A retired Head Mistress, a Teacher, an Architect, an Accountant; there were Sisters, Nuns, a priest and even a fashion magazine editor from London, a really diverse group.

Basically, it was four full days of deep meditation, with both morning and then afternoon sessions.

Confidentiality stops me telling exactly what happened, however the general idea of the first three days was to remove any blocks or hurts that may be present within the mind. Once cleansed we would then be able to gain access into the 'Inner Child'. It was a form of conditioning oneself ready for the final day devoted to connecting with the 'Inner Child'.

The programme started on the Monday and immediately one by one at regular intervals one of us would become, what I can only describe as being 'struck down'. It can only, on reflection, be described as a kind of healing, a release, a removing of a blockage, so allowing the flow of energy fighting to come out, to be released. In some cases, not all, it was like watching someone having their teeth pulled out without anaesthetic, very painful whilst it was happening but then followed by a great sense of relief.

After we had been meditating for nearly two days I felt it just wasn't touching me; I was expecting more (I did get more but not until later on in the week). I caught one of the sisters and told her how I felt, and she said, "It's because you are already there, Robert. You and three others, you are already where all the others want to be."

She went on to say something quite astounding: "You can achieve more in a three-minute prayer than most can in hours." Well, did that give me something to think about! It turned out to be this very same technique that you are now reading about.

Strangely enough though, it was really uncanny; because there I was, sitting in on a group session with a group of total strangers (apart from Maurice), watching exactly the same thing that I was studying with my hypnotherapy course. What would normally only have been seen in a one to one situation, I was able to witness within a group session.

To my knowledge this was the first time that this type of workshop had been attempted and I could see why; they must have had concerns because the atmosphere was always electrifying. You just didn't know what was going to happen next, or who with.

The Final Day
The final day came and all the preparations for this day were now complete. The meditation to connect with and unite with the 'Inner Child' commenced. It was a very long session and I now will relate my own personal experience of what happened during this meditation.

It started like most other meditations; with a breathing exercise and then imagining being in a pleasant meadow on a sunny day. Once the feeling of being relaxed had settled in, then to imagine walking gently out of the meadow, climbing up a gentle hill.

Then the first surprise, it turned out that I was going to be introduced to my spiritual Guide. Now up to this point I wasn't aware I actually had a spiritual Guide. At the same time I was aware of my breathing pattern; breathing in and out, steadily, and aware of being in this lovely, calm, beautiful place. I had this sense, a sense of being touched on my arm, I honestly felt it, I had been touched, and then from then onwards I felt I wasn't alone. Actually it was quite a pleasant feeling. When I asked my companion her name she said "Moea".

We came to the entrance of a very large building, very much like a museum with large pillars, and then we climbed up several steps and through the large doors. We then had entered into a very large hall with high ceilings. Here I spent some time just looking around. It was really strange because I felt I was there, by now I was no longer connected in any shape or form with the room I was sitting in.

It really was strange because I could really see objects like ornate pottery of animals and birds, the detail was so sharp, the vision so crystal clear, the colours so real.

When we were ready, we proceeded along through the hall into a very long corridor, like a corridor in a large hotel, well lit and carpeted, although this was the longest corridor that I had ever seen. All the way along this corridor were doors on both sides. We started to walk down this corridor and after a while opened a door on the right and entered into a dimly lit room, the size of a lounge in an average house.

In this room I could see there was a table, which looked more like a stone altar, the kind you would find in old churches. On the table there was a statue of a small child standing facing away from me. Now this was beginning to become quite emotional, I just didn't know what to expect next. As I moved nearer and nearer the statue of the small child began to turn round so I could see his face. Then the next big surprise as there was this remarkable change when the statue came to life. It wasn't a statue any longer but a real small child.

I was now looking straight into his eyes and just for a few seconds that look spoke volumes, it was a loving, knowing look, a reassuring look, and everything was relaxed, everything at peace. It was so emotional so safe I could feel the tears just streaming down from my eyes and I didn't know why. Whilst there in this pleasant peaceful state I reflected on all the things I had experienced, all the people, family and friends who had been involved to get me to this moment in time.

I became aware of a lifetime of thoughts. I can only imagine likening it to a drowning man when, it is said, all his life flashes before him, but I wasn't drowning. Then for a little while we talked to each other. I was having a meaningful conversation; I was asking questions but more importantly I was being given meaningful answers.

Then, out of the blue was another surprise, suddenly and at first I hadn't even noticed it was so natural, but we had stopped talking and our conversation had switched to telepathy. There aren't words to describe these feelings; it was truly an amazing experience one I wouldn't have missed for the world.

For a time it was like watching a film with me in it and yet as I was watching I didn't know, I didn't have a clue was going to happen next.

Our conversation carried on at a telepathic level of mind so clearly, so easily. It was like watching a play within a play. I then noticed that my cupped hands were lit up. It was like having a light bulb in your hands in a darkened room. I could see a light through my closed-cupped hands.

I didn't know what to expect next, I just watched in amazement as my hands gently opened revealing a small light that then slowly floated up. It looked like the flame of a candle. I continued to watch it slowly float up and away towards the corner of the room and then it started to sway gently round the room, it reminded me of 'Tinker Bell' in Peter Pan. It then moved from side to side, and then it started to come back closer and closer until it came so close it just vanished as if through my forehead. In fact that's what I thought: it had entered into my head.

It seemed so real I was surprised that I hadn't felt anything. However, the sense of the occasion was now becoming so overwhelming, and yet truly wondrous. I was experiencing a very deep inner peace, a total calm mixed with anticipation.

"Ask your inner Child your life's purpose", said a voice that I recognised as that of one of the sisters, conducting the meditation. *"It will tell you."* There was by now a real deep feeling of emotion and more tears, as I knew this question was about to be answered. Although I was conscious and aware, I didn't feel as though I was awake. Then the answer came back and I was overwhelmed.

Then after a moment of silence I was invited to step out through another door into a beautiful garden alone, a peaceful very safe garden. I sat down to reflect on all that had happened, in the other room, in the building, in my life, Moira, my wife, all my friends and family.

Strangely I was aware that there was another exit from this garden, other than the way I had come in. Maybe the less said about this the better. However there was something very unusual about that garden, it's a kind of code known only to a few people who have been there and those who have had out of body experiences will know, and it's this: the garden wasn't green. It was all in glorious white.

After what seemed to be another lifetime, and when I was ready and it felt right, I went back into the room where my 'Inner Child' was waiting. Along with my spiritual guide I said good bye and we slowly left.

Then we retraced all our steps back down the long corridor and back into the main hall. Then we went towards the entrance and out and down several steps and then back down the mountainside. I said an emotional 'goodbye' to Moea, my spiritual guide, and went along through a meadow and finally came back into the present, the here and now.

It was now, for the first time, I was once again aware that there were other people in that room with me. I was now fully back in mind, body and spirit, back in the Cenacle. Everyone seemed to have the same look of disbelief, of amazement, of surprise. It was like wakening up from a dream only I could remember every minute detail. Although it's now many years later, I can still remember every detail.

Once again, one of the sisters spoke. "You can now visit your 'Inner Child' whenever you want to, you can go to your special garden now at will, now you have found the way." Over the years I have made many such visits.

One of the sisters asked, "Did you ask your Inner Child what was your life's purpose?" and "What were you told?"

Imagine this: we were all sitting in this very large circle and the sisters started by asking the person two places to my right, which meant I was about to hear everybody else's 'Life's Purpose' before they heard mine.

"What was your purpose?" She went round the circle anti-clockwise asking everybody what he or she had been told. Most replied with a single word. It was surprising, without exception each had been told something. I was listening very carefully as I thought there would be many who would have the same reply. I couldn't believe it but no one else had been told the same as me. When it was my turn, I said, "I was told **'Healing'**, that's what I was told." My life's mission. No wonder when I demonstrate crystal healing, then, that I seem to get such good results.

Maybe I am fulfilling my destiny, after all there are many forms of healing, and maybe this helps to explain why I am doing what I do. Why I give talks on the mysteries surrounding Gemstones and Crystals and why I write books on the subject and why I make 'Themed Power Bracelets', especially when the 'Healer' bracelet is proving to be so popular. Maybe it's because for many they do actually work and you are about to learn of an explanation that explains the how and why.

I haven't forgotten about my neighbour Maurice. He had a brilliant week. When we left to drive back home to Yorkshire, he didn't say a word for at least three hours, but he did have a permanent smile fixed onto his face.

Further explanations
In searching for the secret Formula we need to explore not so much what we don't know, but more what we do know.

Let me ask you a question: can you ride a bike? This question is not as daft as it may sound. What was the difference from when you couldn't ride a bike to the time when you could? I think the difference is 'knowing'. You somehow know you can. It took me three days to learn how to ride a bike. Do you know how I learnt; I fell off, however on the third day something must have happened because I stayed on and I have stayed on ever since.

Another example of this 'knowing' is driving a car. Look at a learner struggling for the first time to learn how to use all the controls, mirrors, brakes and at the same time dealing with navigating through all the traffic, it's one horrendous nightmare. It's daunting for the most experienced of drivers let alone a learner, and yet look at them again say three months after they have passed their driving test. Cruising down a motorway; listening to the radio, holding a conversation with their passengers and even maybe on the phone. Something has certainly happened. So for the moment let's just say they 'know' they can. And it's this 'knowing' that we are interested in.

It doesn't matter how long you have watched someone swim, you just can't learn to swim by watching. You have to experience it and get into the water, and when you can take your feet off the floor and swim it's then that this knowing kicks in. My wife tells me it's the same with touch typing; once the knowing kicks in it all becomes automatic and effortless.

Let me introduce you to a picture. What you are about to see is no trick or illusion. In fact what you are about to experience probably in about thirty seconds is this 'knowing', the very same 'knowing' that allowed me to ride a bike, drive a car, swim and even type. It's called Leeper's Ambiguous Lady.

It was also called 'My Wife My Mother-in-Law'

Leeper's Ambiguous Lady
What do you see? An attractive young lady or an old witch?
Whatever you see - you see; but keep looking, don't turn away,
and you will shortly experience your 'knowing' kicking in.
Objectively they are both in the picture,
but it is impossible to see them both together.

Have you seen? If you're not sure, look at the picture again. If you saw a young looking woman, as 80% of most audiences in the UK do, then look at the choker around her neck. That is the mouth of the older women, the chin is the nose and the ear is the eye.

However, if you saw the older women first, the one that looks a little like a witch, I can tell you from years of experience, that it might be more difficult for you to see the younger women. She is in profile and on her right side you'll see her nose and eyelash. The eye of the old women becomes her ear and the nose of the old women becomes her chin and the mouth becomes her neck and a choker. The picture first appeared in Puck in 1915 and has been well used in psychology.

In my presentations, I use this picture to great effect; it's a way of introducing people to this 'knowing', to show that there is something more, something they hadn't expected. It's a great way of making the point that things are not always as you would expect them to be.

We are used to living and seeing things in our 'conscious' world, and that's how it should be. Your 'conscious' mind acts like the gatekeeper; it controls what's going in. So in this case it is a picture that you saw, whichever one you saw. However your 'subconscious' mind can see the other, opposite, picture and now can't make up its mind as to which picture you should be seeing. So it will start to fluctuate between the two. **It is this experience which will guide us to the key to finding the secret ingredient.**

It's always interesting when there are two people sitting next to each other who cannot agree on what they are seeing, although they are both looking at the same picture. Why not ask your family and friends to see what they see, you could be surprised.

A Town women's Guild
I remember one evening at a Town Women's Guild where there were eighteen ladies in the room. The Chairperson had brought her daughter that evening, for the first time, to the meeting, as she wanted to hear my talk on the mysteries surrounding Gemstones and Crystals, a talk called 'Crystal Power – Fact or Fiction?'. Her daughter, who would probably have been in her late 40's, could only see the young woman. But the interesting thing was her mother could only see the older woman. In fact that night everybody saw the young women first with only the chairperson being the exception.

I have never heard two women argue so much over a picture. The mother could only see the old woman and her daughter could only see the young woman. "She's young!" shouted the daughter. "No she isn't!" shouted back her mother, "she looks like a witch." And the arguing just went on and on.

Then it was like a miracle, they both saw the other picture at the same time. There was this air of both shock and excitement. The silence was deafening, for the first time in their lives, they realised that they saw some things differently. The chairperson came up to me afterwards and asked what it meant, because she was the only one who, at first, saw the old woman. "Well it means, thank goodness you were there," I said.

One of the patterns that has emerged over the years, at least in the UK, is that there is never more than one third of any audience that can see the old women first. The majority of any group always sees the young women first, just as I do.

Imagine two people sitting facing each other, and one holds up a coin and says, "I can see it's tails on my side, what do you see?" Now you can only see one side of a coin at a time, so the other person would see heads. Although they can both describe the same coin, they are actually seeing it differently. Like the difference of watching the same film but one sees it in colour whilst the other watches it in black and white.

Amazingly, nature seems to sort this out automatically. That's why they say opposites attract. The vast majority of us are never made aware of this fascinating knowledge and so can never appreciate the tremendous powers that have been made available to us. However, once we have been made aware, using this knowledge enables us to achieve whatever definite aims, goals and ambitions we have for the future. This is part of our 'Power Pack', our 'survival kit'.

Let's change tack - what if it's not the Crystal
but the belief in the Crystal?

Now we have, with the help of Leeper's Ambiguous Lady discovered, our 'knowing', we are ready to move on to discover the next lesson and learn about a little known formula. A formula which is Biblically based.

I am going to put into words an explanation that you would not normally hear. It's an explanation that I believe can explain why Crystal Healing works. First of all let me tell you a story about a friend of mine called Ann. Ann wittered and moaned that she couldn't sleep. She wittered and moaned so much that I took pity on her, and made her a special bracelet. I called it 'Sleep Well', and I gave it to her. Ann said, "But what do I do with it?" "Wear it," I said, "it's programmed," and she did.

I saw Ann several days later and I could see she was wearing her bracelet but she never said anything. I was curious. "Why haven't you mentioned your bracelet, Ann?" I asked. Her answer was a little surprising. "I daren't," she replied. "How do you mean you daren't?" I asked. "I don't want it to stop working," she replied. Now that spoke volumes. It was the same with a 'Fertility' bracelet I made for a young lady who was having some difficulty in starting a family. Could you imagine the conversation when she became pregnant and said it was down to me!

Over the years I have got used to it, the letters, emails and phone calls all saying the same thing, how they have benefited from Gemstones and Crystals, how they would never have believed it if they hadn't experienced it for themselves.

To understand what I am about to say, it's best if I can give you an 'anchor', something that the mind can relate to. Have you ever heard of the 'placebo effect?'(It's *a positive therapeutic effect from an inactive substance administered to a patient who insists on receiving medication or who would benefit by the psychological deception).*

Although it's based on a lie, it must be the most natural form of healing known to man, with absolutely no side effects. Now what would you do if you knew how that worked?

So you now know that I am describing the placebo effect.

I could talk about Quantum physics or the Molecular structure but it wouldn't probable make any sense to most of us, so I will let this story about a fourteen year old girl explain it. She explains it much better than I ever could.

The Formula
She came home one day with a face like 'thunder'. "I've no chance, he's the most popular boy in the year, will he look at me, will he heck," (a true Yorkshire expression) "my clothes don't fit, I'm overweight and I've got spots." She was full of verbal diarrhoea. When she had calmed down: from her adolescent teenage rant. It was suggested that there was a formula that just might help her. Did she know that **'when imagination and willpower are in conflict, imagination will always win, and it's set in granite?** And then she was told how to use it.

Well it must have worked because about three weeks later she came home from school with her face beaming from side to side. He had asked her out and apparently all the girls now wanted to know what she had been told, I bet they did. Except Celia, apparently she was going round school telling everybody that I must be a witch. "Who's Celia?" I asked. "Her father is a local minister," she replied. Oh! Heck (that great Yorkshire expression again), now am I in bother.

Before I tell you what she had been instructed to do with the formula, let me tell you another true story about using this very same formula.

Our Coach Trip
I have regularly gone on holidays to Spain with my wife Moira. And we have often travelled by coach, we both enjoy coach travel, and it does extend the holiday by at least two to three days. This particular year was the year I was doing all the research into the mysteries surrounding gemstones and crystals, and over the years this has proved to be quite significant. It was the year when I demonstrated for myself and with a witness the awesome power of this 'formula'.

Every year when we had gone abroad by coach, the courier's always seemed to sell raffle tickets for £1, presumably to earn a little extra from the passengers. These coaches were always those double-deckers that you see around Europe and probably carried around sixty to seventy passengers including two drivers and a courier. I bought a ticket and on this occasion it came over on the 'tannoy' that the first prize was a 'Magnum of Champagne' and the second prize two bottles of wine. I turned to Moira and said "I'll show you the magic, I'll show you how to win, and so what do you think?" Before she had chance to answer I continued, "I don't fancy the champagne but I do fancy the two bottles of wine. Go on,.what do you think?"

"I think you're crackers," was her reply, "it's got to you hasn't it, all this reading and research, it's time for you to have a holiday." But I was going on holiday, and not only that, I won the two bottles of wine.

But this story didn't end there, because two weeks later when we were travelling home on a different coach with a different courier, this courier decided to play 'bingo'. Now I don't like 'bingo', I find it far too stressful. However I bought a card and turned to Moira, saying, "I'll show you again the magic, I'll show you how to win." She replied, "I don't know how you did it last time Robert, but you have no chance," and she said it quite dismissively. "You watch," I angrily replied, I was annoyed that she wasn't taking me seriously enough. I suppose on reflection I did sound quite arrogant.

What happened next was actually scary, because the numbers being called were just filling my card row after row, and then finally I only needed one number for a full house – and she then called it, it was a number 14. I had won! - I couldn't believe it and from the look on Moira's face, neither could she. Especially after what had just been said about winning. In fact on this occasion I had been so concerned about the winning that I had forgotten to take note of the winning prize. That turned out to be a pack of twenty four lagers. I nearly got a hernia trying to carry them and our suitcases, after we were dropped off to find a taxi.

Now what are the chances of winning both times, when you have said in advance that you will? Is it all a coincidence, or is there something else at play?

Back to our fourteen year old girl. What I would have liked to have said to her was, "Well why don't you pray?" and if I had said that there was no doubt in my mind I wouldn't have seen her again, she wouldn't have taken any notice, however I did, I did tell her how to pray only she didn't know I had. Sometimes a little sub diffusion can prove to be quite useful, think of the 'placebo effect'.

I suggested that she drew a heart on a piece of paper and she put her initials and his initials onto it.

Fold it up and place it close to her heart, then as often as she could, take it out, open it up, look at it; and then I wanted her to do something she had just said was impossible. Could she imagine him asking her out? Not the other way around; that would be cheating. "Yes I am always doing that." "Well how would you 'feel' if he did ask you out?" "Oh, marvellous!" she said. "There you are then, that's the key, turn it."

Well he did ask her out and they went out for over four weeks. Then do you know what happened? She ditched him.

With my wife on the coach it was the same formula. I had imagined hearing my wife saying "You've won again Robert," and I don't win that often, I only wished I did. Then I imagined how I would feel if I did. Yessssss! whilst punching the air in my imagination. It seems to make a difference. Some people would say I am talking about a 'positive mental attitude' and in a way I am but it wasn't where I was coming from.

In my quest to understand and to help explain this formula, a formula that I think goes a long way to explaining the placebo effect, I have been guided to read some fascinating books, I have heard of some great theories and all the while I have tried to keep an open mind. I was not only drawn to this passage in the Bible but also the formula that arrived shortly afterwards. When I say arrived I don't mean by post, I mean it arrived in my mind my thoughts:- *When imagination and willpower are in conflict, imagination will always win, and it's set in granite.*

Mark 11:22 Therefore I tell you, whatever you ask for in prayer, believe that you have received it, and it will be yours.

How do you believe you have received something? Easy, imagine you have got it, but here is the 'key, the code, the secret': you must add a feeling, an emotion.

There is a coded language out there and when you know this code it's so simple. Whenever I hear someone say, 'you won't believe this,' or, 'that's strange,' or, 'I was thinking about you,' or. 'that's a coincidence,' I always listen to what comes next. That's the code for the power at work.

I was walking through my home town of Huddersfield on a Friday afternoon when I seemed to have a brain-storm What a lovely way to finish my talks, I thought; if only I could find that picture. So I went into a specialised book/gift shop and I described this picture I was looking for. "I know what you mean," he replied, and then the bomb shell, "but I haven't a clue where you will get it." Now I walked out of that shop honestly feeling disappointed. I really thought it was a great idea and wouldn't have any problems finding it. I really thought I was on a 'roll'.

Saturday came and I could still feel this disappointment, it just didn't seem to go away. It was still there on Sunday but by Monday, thankfully, it had gone. Life had taken over and I forgot all about it. Until Monday tea time when my daughter came in from work, although I was only half listening, she was saying that her friend had been to a car boot sale on the Sunday and had bought what she thought was a very unusual tapestry.

It was so unusual that my daughter had thought it might be of interest to me. "Here, have a look," she said. "I have tried to draw a picture for you," and so I looked, and then did I look; it was the very same picture that I had gone into a shop for on the Friday afternoon and had asked about, and I promise you nobody on earth had known that that's what I had done. If that's not a coincidence, I don't know what is.

Have fun with the picture. It's your 'knowing' that will see it first and then show it to you. It has to, it's 'Universal Law'.

It was a perfect day
Elaine said:
"How do you know there's a God?"
"That's simple," I said, "There is a code;
Understand the code, and you can see the power of God."

Look at Luke 8:10, where Jesus says:

> The Knowledge of the secret
> of the kingdom of God has been
> given to you, but to others
> I speak in parables, so that
> *though seeing, they may not see;*
> *though hearing, they may not understand.*

It started when my wife and I came back home from our summer holidays, and our eldest daughter, along with her partner, collected us from the airport.

"We've got some good news for you!" she said. "We're going to get married. And we have decided to combine the wedding and the honeymoon. We're going to the Caribbean Island of the Dominican Republic."

Over the next few months, the wedding started to be planned; there were a lot of documents and details that needed sorting out. Then we thought: wouldn't it be nice if the mothers could be there, even if it was only for a week ....Why not a fortnight, as the main expense is the cost of the flights..? And what about the fathers, wouldn't they like to come!

We couldn't all get into the same hotel as my eldest daughter – and anyway, we were reminded, it was to be her honeymoon – but we did manage to get booked into another hotel just five minutes away. It was on one of those complexes where there is a group of all-inclusive hotels, which seem to cater for this kind of Caribbean wedding. Five star, no less.

So the six of us – my wife and I and our youngest daughter, along with my future son-in-law's mother and father and their daughter – all arrived at Manchester Airport late February 2001, at around seven in the morning, for the start of a perfect day.

We were two hours late setting off due to a very heavy snow storm. At times it was so thick that it was just like trying to see through fog.
"What code?" Elaine asked again.
The diplomatic services and other groups of professionals seem to have their own way of communicating with each other using a special coded language, only known within their own profession.

I discovered, during my research, that God has such a code, and it is simply this: that whenever I heard someone say the following words: You won't believe this, but ... or: How strange ... or: What a coincidence ... or: I was thinking of you, when ... or: It was so perfect, it was weird ... I would stop whatever I was doing, and then deliberately listen to whatever was said next.

Because whatever comes next is always, almost without exception, an indication of God's power at work.

Now, because we have 'Free Will' we can easily dismiss giving credit to the power of God by simply calling it a coincidence, or 'how strange', or 'you won't believe this', etc. So I am always on the lookout for what you could call coincidences. *A **Coincidence:** A chance occurrence of events remarkable either for being simultaneous or for apparently being connected.*

Let's go back to the airport and the snow storm. The flight originated from Gatwick Airport and was delayed landing because of the snow. The jet, my wife noticed, was named Sir Matt Busby MBE. We boarded the plane and took our seats. The pilot then announced that because of the ice now forming on the wings, he was wasn't prepared to take off until the plane had been de-iced, and had ordered a de-icing crew to come along; which they did, eventually, and we took off about two hours late.

My wife reminded us all, later, that the 'Busby Babes' – the Manchester United football team – had crashed in a plane in 1957 because of ice on the plane. It was no wonder the pilot didn't want to take off with snow and ice still on the plane.

On a much lighter note, we arrived on the island early evening, benefiting from a four-hour time gain. The holiday couriers met us, and we were bussed into the complex just about 20-30 minutes later. On the journey, it became obvious just how poor this country was, although just starting to develop. People were living in shanty-type huts; the rough road we were travelling on was considered to be their motorway, but to us in Britain it wouldn't even have been a 'B' road. We were also led to believe they didn't have to take driving tests, they just drove!

It was pointed out to us just how much sugar cane there was on the island, and that the majority of it was consumed by the islanders themselves, being either turned into their renowned white rum with a very high proof, or added to their vehicles as fuel.

First impressions
Our first impressions on this occasion were wrong. We felt we had arrived into a type of 1950's Butlins Holiday Camp: however, these first impressions quickly vanished after our first full day.

My wife, Moira, jokingly said how it reminded her of that parody, years ago: 'Hello Mother, Hello Father, here we are at Camp Granada'. Although we tried, at the time we couldn't remember the exact words, but we remembered that at the end it said something like 'it's stopped raining, things are better, so please disregard this letter.'

We first met Elaine when she became friendly with our daughter. She had been unfortunate in boarding at Gatwick, which because of the delays had made her journey hours longer than ours. She had two weeks off work and had decided to go away on her own.

Elaine was brilliant. She had made up her mind to go on everything and anything, if she could; 'you only live once' seemed to be her motto for the fortnight. She went on safaris, she went horse-riding with my daughter just to keep her company, as my daughter likes horse-riding but didn't want to go on her own. Elaine went on a catamaran, whale watching, shooting the rapids; she was brilliant to listen to because in the evening when she came back she would describe in great detail how she had gone on.

We were all spellbound just listening to her, and the effect on the rest of us was that she saved us money. Why? Because after listening to her, we felt we had already been and done it. We were able to live through her experiences.

Remember God's special code ...
The day before the wedding was a little worrying from the point of view of the weather. It was very untypical: cloudy all day, and even raining quite a bit. We heard that all the weddings that day were held inside, and it must have been very disappointing for those who had gone for the weather.

It was a relief that on the day of our family's wedding the skies were blue. We all arrived at their hotel early, had breakfast with them and then sunbathed for an hour or so before returning to our hotel – which was only five minutes away – to get dressed more formally for the day. When the sun was out it was probably approaching the nineties, so we welcomed the site of some white clouds passing over, offering some shade.

The wedding was at 2.30. I was very proud to escort my daughter past the huge swimming pool, down towards the beach end of the complex, to a gazebo all nicely decorated for the occasion. My daughter was wearing a typical English white wedding dress with a tiara. I think she had decided to make more of the dress because of the family being there. On the day she looked just like a princess (but there again, what else would a proud father think).

Now, I had thought we would go past the swimming pool quite discreetly, but it soon became very apparent how wrong I was. The moment we left their accommodation block, which was at the side of the pool, the hotel tannoy system started blaring out the Wedding March. There were hundreds of mainly Americans and Canadians, all sunbathing, and when they heard the Wedding March being played they all looked, and then began to stand, and then they started to clap.

They were saying things like 'Congratulations!' and 'Well done!' and 'Are you British?' all in their American accents. There were more photos taken, and the number of videos we must be on ....!

Here are the **coincidences.** The guitarists played my son-in-law's father his favourite song, which made him feel quite emotional – then the next song turned out to be my daughter's and her about-to-be husband's favourite song. Although it was 'their song' nobody had told the guitarists what to play. **How strange** that it just happened. **You won't believe** what happened next. Three of us were all taking pictures with our cameras, me, my youngest daughter and their daughter, when all three cameras ran out of film at preciously the same time – you could clearly hear all of them rewinding at the same moment.

Everyone agreed at the end of the day how everything had just **been perfect**. And how about this for a coincidence: I had bought the Daily Mail (I only bought three papers all holiday, mainly because they cost so much) and I was reading the Q and A section they have, where you can ask anything you want and somebody will write back with an answer. QUESTION: What are the full words to Camp Granada (Hello Mudda, Hello Fadda)?

I showed it to my wife, who said, **"I can't believe** this, we were only talking about it just a few days ago. It must be over 40 years since this parody was recorded- **what a coincidence'**.

On the last day Elaine said, **'You won't believe** this, but this holiday **has just been perfect.'**

Then she looked at me in amazement
as she realised what she had just said.

Another coincidence!
On the 5th October, my son got married; he had asked me if I would help him by videoing his wedding, using a camera he had hired. During the next few days, we discussed what it would take to video one of my talks; a camera, lighting, sound, editing etc. etc.

On the 17th October, I was invited to give a talk for a fundraising group, raising money for the 'Macmillan Nurses'. After we had arranged a date, the one who was organising the event asked if I would mind if they videoed my presentation. It was going to be a project for their 'Cine club' as one of their members had just acquired a £3,000 Sony Editing Unit and they wanted a project for them to work on through the winter months. Wow! You could have knocked me down with a feather, but what a coincidence. By the following Easter and after six months of them filming and editing, they presented me with my very own 'promotional' video'.

We all have a 'Power' that's beyond imagination

Have you ever gone to answer the phone and thought you knew who it was before you answered it, and then realised you were right? It happens a lot in families, it's called 'telepathy' and I think it's brought about by the person phoning, who at the same time, is thinking about who they are phoning, they imagine that person. If this is done with 'feeling' then this seems to trigger this effect known as 'telepathy'. This 'telepathy' works just as well, whether the call comes from across the road or from the other side of the world. It can travel the globe, faster than dialling the number.

Did you know that electricity travels almost as fast as the speed of light? In fact it's so fast it can travel the globe almost seven times per second.

If you ever saw the film Crocodile Dundee, there was a part where Crocodile Dundee summons help by producing a weight on the end of a piece of string and then by swinging it around above his head which produced different sounds just like a bee buzzing. Maybe we were meant to believe that the Aborigines are exceptionally good at hearing, they don't need phones, but isn't this another example of 'telepathy', if you realise that just as the message was being sent, it was also being imagined?

People regularly ask me how they can connect with their crystals.

The answer is quite simple: let them excite your imagination either by their colour, touch or the mysteries that surrounds them. Then imagine how you would 'feel' when they work. How do you know if you are connected? Well if you lost them, would you miss them? and if the answer is yes, then you are connected. Imagine a happy ending, finding a solution to your or someone else's problem. Feel the thrill, really feel it, the thrill of accomplishment, and once what you have imagined and felt is accepted by both your mind and your subconscious mind, it will bring it to pass.

Knowledge of this 'knowing', this power within the subconscious mind is the beginning of the road to all kinds of amazing riches and contentment.

It is everybody's right to discover this inner world of thought, feelings and mighty power. Understand that as soon as the subconscious mind accepts an idea, it proceeds immediately to put it into effect.

Once we have realised that the 'Power' that moves the world and the Universe, is also moving on our behalf, we then cease believing in false beliefs, opinions, superstitions and other fears that 'haunt' mankind.

By believing in the eternal virtues and the 'Truths of Life', the ones that never change, our confidence and assurance just grows and grows.

Maybe it's not the 'thing' believed in but the 'belief' within the mind which brings about the positive results. Know that whatever you imagine and imagine as true, will and must, as a 'Law of Life', come to pass.

Know this: that a man does NOT heal by a different power than that of another, even though he may think his own theory or method is different. So find the method or theory that's right for you.

Wherever you are on your journey through life, there will, when you need it, be someone or something that will be willing and able to help.

So go in Peace, Live Long and Prosper
oOo

Finding it difficult to acquire Gemstones and Crystals? We have a free search and find division with worldwide contacts.

For further details:-
Email - info@rosewood-gifts.co.uk

For the very latest information, why not visit our web site:
www.rosewood-gifts.co.uk

About the Author

Robert W Wood D.Hp, was born November 25th 1948, in Huddersfield, West Yorkshire, England. A committed Christian who has discovered a very interesting gift, he seems to be able to take 'church' language and change it to 'New Age'.

He was confirmed into the Church of England at the age of 38. Never having had any kind of indoctrination into any kind of religion up to this point, he was truly a 'blank sheet of paper'.

Whilst sitting in a church in 1988, he was told – through his mind – that once the service ended he should not move, because something was about to happen. What Robert did not know was just how far-reaching this something was going to be.

That day, in church, he met a man who was about to become a very special friend to him. This man, a fellow Christian, was the owner of the largest wholesalers in the UK selling fossils, minerals and semi-precious gemstones. Although Robert did not realise it at the time, it was the start of a complete change of direction for him, his nexus.

Within his mind he experienced a strong feeling of being awakened as he was given more details of his life's mission, to de-mystify the Mysteries. Taking as his starting-point the idea: "Why try to predict the future, when you are the one who can change it?" he came to make it his quest. Those thoughts gave him the inspiration to produce his book 'Astrology the Secret Code', incorporating the little known - 'The Law of Polarity'.

For many years he has been giving talks and displays on the mysteries surrounding Gemstones and Crystals, including, quite effectively, demonstrations on Crystal Healing with great results.

Quite unique, don't you think: a committed Christian talking 'New Age', and the same person also a qualified 'Hypnotherapist'. This unique personal combination has brought about this book 'Why Crystal Healing Works' – an emotive title, but if you heard Robert give one of his talks, you would realise just how electrifying his presentations are.

The church's differing views.
You may think, as I did, that the 'church' would have a straight forward view or at least a standard reply to the subject of crystals and gemstones. However, I have discovered over many years that not all churches seem to *sing from the same hymn sheet'*. For example: one church may openly embrace new ideas, whilst another defiantly won't. Many use candles, but some deliberately don't. Most use real wine for Communion, but some will only use substitutes or non-alcoholic wine.

Some churches will use 'rice paper' as a bread substitute, while others will only use fresh bread (I used to be the one who got the crust, so I must say I like the rice paper). Most are quite relaxed regarding raffles – many churches I know use raffles or tombolas to raise small fortunes for all kinds of good causes – but some churches still frown upon it.

I first came across 'the Church's view' when I received a phone call from a woman one Thursday evening. She said she was ringing to let me know that although I was due to give a talk to their Pensioners Group the following Monday, one of the elders in the church that they used for their meetings had seen one of my posters, and had complained to the Minister that it wasn't right for such a talk to be given on Church property. I believe she had objected to the word 'Astrology'. On the poster, amongst other things, it said 'Discover a connection between **Astrology** and the Scriptures'. So from then on all the posters then said, 'Discover a connection between **Birthstones** and the Scriptures' and after that change most complaints just seemed to melt away.

Back to the woman on the phone; so I said, "are you ringing then to cancel the talk? "Oh, no!" she replied, "It's just that the Minister has asked us whether in this case, if we wouldn't mind, could we have our meeting in the Civic Centre that's next to the church. The Civic Centre actually costs more, but the church will cover the extra expense. So, Mr Wood, I'm just ringing to ask if, on Monday, you would go straight to the Civic Centre where the caretaker will be glad to meet you and let you in, instead of going to the church."

Monday arrived. I set up my display of various gemstone and crystal gifts including some jewellery, in the hall and eventually everyone arrived. It turned out to be quite a turnout. Apparently word had got round, and I was led to believe that there were a lot more of the church's parishioners there than usual, so I suspect many may have come out of curiosity! The organiser asked if I would say a word to explain why they were meeting in the Civic Centre and not the church.

"I would be delighted to," I said. "It's called 'hypocrisy'. Apparently you can't hear me in the church – but you can hear me in the Civic Hall. Not only that, but the church is paying so you can use the Hall, since it works out more expensive than using the church!"

Here's a surprise, some weeks later I received a call from a Ladies Group, booking my talk. When I asked where they met, it turned out to be at the same church! "I can't," I said, half joking, "I've been banned from there," "I know," she replied, "so we have decided not to tell them that you're coming." And so, a few weeks later, I did give my talk in the very same church.

A short while afterwards I was speaking at another church of the same denomination. After the talk I noticed a poster on their noticeboard advertising a Halloween Party. Casually, I asked if they rented the room out "Oh, no," was the reply, "that's us, the church, we're having the party." I hope she didn't see in my face, my surprise. It was the same denominational church, but with different views.

At around eight o'clock one Sunday evening I received a phone call from a woman, asking me to confirm that everything was okay for me to give my talk the following Thursday evening. I said yes, everything was fine and I was looking forward to seeing her there. Apparently she was the one who had recommended me, after hearing me give my talk at another group that she went to.

Thirty minutes later the phone rang again, and this time it was the Vicar ringing from the same church.

He introduced himself and then went on to say he understood that I had been asked to give my talk to the Mothers Union the following Thursday, and that the talk was called 'Discover the Hidden Powers of Gemstones'. (These days it's called 'Crystal Power – Fact or Fiction?') I confirmed it. He then said, "I'd rather you didn't because I don't want my parishioners coming to church on Sunday morning clutching crucifixes and crystals."

I was a little taken aback, to say the least; in over eight years this was the first time a Vicar had rung and complained. To put his mind at rest, I said, "But it's a Christian-based talk, although it's not intended to be religious."

"How do you mean?" he asked, and without waiting for an answer proceeded to 'grill' me, and started by asking which church I went to. Now as it happens, I was confirmed into the Church of England, the same as his church. He wouldn't let it go. He then named one or two people he knew, to see if I knew them. I ask you, does anybody know the names of the other people you might meet in church? Because I didn't – so it seemed, I'd failed his test. This only encouraged him even more to continue with what turned out to be quite a grilling; fifteen minutes later I was becoming a little annoyed, and at that point I said – I don't even know why I said it, but in fact I shouted at him – **"Luke 9:49".**

"Wait a minute, my Bible's open at the next page," (what a surprise) the Vicar replied. After reading the passage he asked me what it meant. "It means I'm the other one," I told him. I had come across this passage a long time ago, and my memory must have pulled it up from deep within my subconscious. Take a moment to read it, and you will appreciate just how apt it is.

Luke 9:49 "Master" ,said John, "we saw a man driving out demons in your name and we tried to stop him, because he is not one of us." "Do not stop him," Jesus said, "for whoever is not against you is for you."

The Vicar then quietened down a little, and I suggested that he should come along and listen to my talk – he might have found it interesting.

"I'm far too busy to do that," he said and then went on to explain his concerns for his parish. Apparently there had once been a ghost hunt organised in his town, and over 600 people had turned up (and I think that at the same time he may have been struggling to get people into his church).

I gave the talk and it turned out okay; my audience all knew that the vicar had rung me, but they chose not to say anything, I did discover that he had sent his wife. Afterwards, many came up to me and told me in private how much they had enjoyed the talk.

Don't get the idea that I am knocking the church – I'm not. What I would say is: if, on your journey through life, you should come across one of these 'characters' with such strong views, don't judge the Church by their standards. These people are becoming rare, although I still come up against then now and again. You will find a lot of warmth, genuine love and a friendly welcome in the majority of Churches.

I came across another one of these 'characters', a woman rang sounding very apologetic and a little embarrassed. I was due to give my talk at her church just a few days later, but she was ringing to cancel. It turned out that the minister had objected very strongly to me giving my talk, leaving her no option but to cancel me. She then went on to say he had also told her not to have anybody giving talks on Yoga or Aromatherapy. After she had told me that, I didn't feel too bad! And from my point of view I did rather well out of it – I actually received three other bookings from the same area as a direct consequence of the minister cancelling me. Strange thing, publicity …!

Here are some extracts from just a selection of the many letters that I receive. Not all of them are complimentary.

The Tuesday Club members were delighted with your talk and presentation ... I overheard a very animated description of your talk being given to two members who missed the meeting! They are hoping you will be doing another presentation in the area in the not too distant future.   United Reformed Church.

Thank you very much indeed for your splendid presentation and talk...
                                                      Methodist Church

Thank you for a very informative and interesting talk on Thursday evening.
                                                      Ladies Group

Just a note to thank you for giving us a super talk, and presentation, on Tuesday. We had our Annual Garden Party yesterday and everyone was still buzzing excitedly about you.   *Women's Institute*

Thank you so much for your very interesting talk on 'The Hidden Powers of Gemstones'. Our members thoroughly enjoyed the evening and we appreciated how much time and effort had gone into the preparation for coming to our meeting. Thank you once again.   *Mothers Union*

... a very interesting subject ...   *Mothers Union*

We all had a very enjoyable evening and feel we know much more about the history and the powers of Gemstones.   *Townswomen's Guild*

On behalf of the members ... may I thank you for coming along to our meeting last Monday ... Our members found the talk very interesting and informative. It was certainly very different to anything we'd heard or seen before.   *Women's Club*

Just in case you think they're all good, then read this one from a church's Mother's Union.

I am writing to cancel the date provisionally made for your talk to us. At our recent committee meeting it was thought to be an inappropriate subject for our Mothers Union meeting.

I wouldn't have minded, but they had rung me to book my talk after someone else had recommended me!

I felt quite vindicated when I received this letter out of the blue:

Dear Robert,
Thank you for the research that you have done to produce a great little book (Astrology the Secret Code) which has helped to settle many arguments. I am a religious education teacher in a Catholic school, a practising Catholic with a degree in history and philosophy. I have been made to feel guilty about my interest in Astrology and Crystals because of my faith, but you have given me some fantastic tools to argue my corner.

Mary

Another interesting letter:
I want to say how fantastic I think your books are and I have read them several times since reading them initially. One particular poignant part I'd like to point out, I found when I read in the last paragraph of the 'Change your Life' book. I realised just how much you really had indeed understood me and my need for direction and truly have allowed me the confidence and strength to know and believe I can achieve whatever I want in life. So I want to thank you from the bottom of my heart – you are an inspiration.

Would you like to help?
We are planning to publish a new book.

We are looking for up-lifting, inspirational, unusual stories.
Anything involving gemstones, crystals or the power of prayer; stories involving coincidences, stories that we could publish.

Have you ever been touched by an angel, had a prayer answered in an unusual way or coincidences that almost 'beggar belief?' If you have such a story we would love to hear from you and if it's suitable we will publish it. Your name and address will, if you wish, remain anonymous.
Keep it as short as possible without losing any impact and email it to:-
info@rosewood-gifts.co.uk
Marking in the subject box "My Story"

Here's an example of some of the stories we are being sent:

Hello my name is ******* I wanted to share my story with you. It's a strange story and maybe I would have doubts if it was someone telling me the story because it's so out of the ordinary, but I was truly saved this night and so I have no doubt in my mind of what occurred.

I had been in a violent relationship with my ex-partner for many years and tried many times to leave; then one day he went too far and I managed to summon the strength to leave. I moved into a women's refuge where I would reside for the next 9 months. My experience had left me no more than a shell of a woman. I suffered from severe anxiety and depression and panic attacks. I cried nearly all day every day. I woke up every morning and the first thing I did was cry because I hadn't died in my sleep. Then one night I was having my usual struggles to sleep because of my panic attacks when the most amazing thing happened. I was lying on my bed with my eyes closed but still awake when suddenly, in my mind's eye, the room filled with light and a beautiful, robed woman sat behind me and placed my head in her lap. She wrapped my blanket around me and stroked my hair and whispered, "sssh, rest now, it will be ok," then she was gone, leaving behind her a lighter, more peaceful and happier air. I fell asleep easily after that and woke up smiling instead of crying. I haven't had a panic attack since that night and although I still take anti-depressants I have been much less depressed since then, too. This happened, and it's still vivid in my mind. I will never forget that day. I truly believe an angel or something was sent to save me. I have never felt so much love as I did that night and I will never forget that when I need them they will help me. An Angel saved my Life.
Name supplied.   Sent from my iPhone.

How's this for a coincidence.
My story.

There is a lovely little café, in the little village of Barley, which is near Pendle Hill, my friend June, myself and another friend went for a country run and a meal to this café, after we had eaten and paid our bill we made our way out, on the way passing the little Tourist Information table and as I was looking at various leaflets on where one could visit, a voice said "Are you thinking of going somewhere nice"? On turning around I saw a middle aged couple who I had never seen before sat at a table, "Oh" I said "I only live about 12 miles away from here, where are you from"? "We are from Australia" was there answer.
"My sister lives there in Geelong, whereabouts do you live"?
"The other side of Melbourne" the lady said.
"My sister's son lives around there, his name is Bobby Clayton" I offered. "Do you know him"?
The lady said "If you are Aunty Win then we are coming to see you on Monday, Bobby is my daughter's boyfriend".
I was absolutely astonished, my flabber was absolutely gasted.
True to what they said, they turned up at our home 12 miles away on the following Monday.
What a Coincidence.

                                                        Winifred Belcher

"My Story"

Hi Robert,
I hope the following 'My Story' will be of interest to you with regard to crystals, synchronicity and the power of healing.

I have had a lifelong fascination with all things metaphysical and crystals in particular. (starting with stones as a child). I was fortunate to complete Reiki training in more recent years whilst continuing to expand my experiences.

The events of "My Story" are as follows:-
I was walking home when I noticed a young Rottweiler dog in a collapsed state on the pavement immediately at my garden gate. The owner explained that her pet could not walk as a result of pain in a hip joint and it transpired this 'collapsed' state occurred on a regular basis after even relatively short walks resulting in the dog having to be carried home. The owners and the poor dog had consequently many sleepless nights as a result of this painful condition. I ascertained that the dog was scheduled for extensive, expensive surgery in the near future. I happened to have a wooden dowser in my pocket and used this to draw out the pain from the joint; I then held its paw and proceeded to apply Reiki Healing for approximately 5-10 minutes. At the end of this time the dog stood on all fours and walked.

As I was at my own garden gate I went into the house and returned with a large piece of Fluorite to give the owner to place under the dog's bedding. It gave me great pleasure to watch them trot along the road, this occurred in 2003. The follow-up is that from that day on the dog has had no trouble walking, the household was never again awakened in the night because of the dogs distress and best of all no surgery was needed.

Wilma Smith.

Another "My Story"

"My Story" concerns the healing of a goldfish. One morning I noticed our goldfish was lying on its side floating on the surface of the water. There was no response to gentle prodding, so I cupped it between my palms under the water, applied Reiki Healing for some time, then felt a flicker of movement. The fish subsequently swam off and survived for another year after this.

Wilma Smith.

Gemstone & Crystal Power – A mystical A to Z of Stones

This book has been written to help those who are interested in alternative treatments, treatments without the side–effects that drugs can have. However, common sense should tell you to see your doctor or practitioner first, before embarking on any kind of alternative treatment. The information that follows is in direct response to those that would like to know more, and is part of a series of books called 'Power for Life' – a series of books based on an ancient wisdom. Keep an open mind and you won't go far wrong.

There are numerous ways of looking into the strange, often mystical world of gemstone and crystal powers, and you'll discover that there are many ways of explaining these mysteries too. I have spent many years researching into all the aspects of crystal power, in the search for a more modern explanation of why, once we are connected to a crystal, that crystal – or the connection – can actually be so beneficial to its user. The following information is only a 'taster' of a very large and complex subject. Before you think of dismissing all this as just hocus-pocus, think about this: at the heart of every computer are silicon chips, and what are they? They're a clear Quartz. A crystal. And crystals have power.

Crystal Power.
According to quantum physics, everything in the universe has an atomic structure – and that includes gemstones and crystals. They contain atomic energy, and this is the most powerful energy known on earth. Others talk of colour frequency. Red, orange and blue may seem to be different colours, but they are in fact all part of the same spectrum of light. Similarly, we tend to think of light, heat and radio waves as being different from each other, but there is a connection. The electromagnetic spectrum represents the complete range of radiation including gamma rays, X-rays, ultraviolet light, visible white light (visible to the human eye), infra-red light, microwaves and radio waves. Just because we can't see it, that doesn't mean it's not there – and it may be the same with gemstones and crystal power.

We can't hear dog whistles, but dogs can; we can't see ultraviolet light, but bees can. Just as our ears can only hear part of the range of possible sounds and cannot hear a dog whistle, so our eyes can only see a small central section of the electromagnetic spectrum of light. The power associated with Gemstones and Crystals falls into this 'can't be seen or heard' category.

How to use the following information.
Within this book you'll find all the information you'll need about the metaphysical, astrological and physical properties of Gemstones, Crystals and minerals. I have scrutinised many sources and cross-referenced all the information to enable me to produce this guide. In short I have done all the work, so that you don't have to.

The best way to use this Guide is to read the full list of Gemstones and Crystals, and at the same time make notes. So, if you are looking for a healing stone for a specific ailment, read the full list, find the stone or stones, and if there are a few, then you might want to narrow them down. There are various ways of narrowing down. Trust your instincts on this one. For instance, you might find, from your research, two gemstones-crystals. It may be that for you, two are ideal. You may be surprised to find that one of the stones is your Birthstone; this would then be the one for you. Or if you have a favourite colour, and if that colour is there on your list, then go with that one. No-one is really sure how all this works; only that, for many, it does. By keeping an open mind – many have been pleasantly surprised.

Colour – and the Chakras.
Another useful guide when choosing crystals could be their colour. In Sanskrit there are original teachings about an energy system known as the 'Chakras'.. When seen clairvoyantly, Chakras are wheels of light and colour. There are seven of them. The first one is found at the base or root – that is, around the base of the spine. The second is the sacral or spleen, the third is the solar plexus, and the fourth is the heart. The fifth is the throat, the sixth is the brow or 'third eye', and the seventh and final one is the crown.

It's said we need all these energy centres to be open so as to enjoy optimum health. Each is associated with a colour; and these colours are the seven colours of the rainbow, and are in the same running order.

Each Chakra is linked with a particular colour in the spectrum of light. The 'root' Chakra is red; the 'sacral' or 'spleen' Chakra is orange; the 'solar plexus' Chakra is yellow; the 'heart' Chakra is green; the 'throat' Chakra is blue; the 'brow' Chakra is indigo; and finally the 'crown' Chakra is violet. I know it all sounds like gobbledygook, but the human body requires light to maintain itself. For example, our bodies produce vitamin D – necessary to make our bones and teeth strong and healthy – and this is increased as a result of exposure to sunlight. Think about this: where does the vitamin D come from? One minute it's not there and the next it is. What makes the difference? Stepping out into sunlight does- so light has a power and you can use this knowledge to your benefit when choosing the right gemstone or crystals.

Cleansing Gemstones and Crystals
Once you have found the right crystals and stones, it's advisable to clean them. This can quite easily be done by placing them under a running tap. Some say they should be washed in salt water; the sea is ideal, but if you're not near the sea then just add some salt to water. Others believe that gemstones and crystals can attract negative energy from other people, and again, cleansing is a way of wiping them clean.

Whichever way you decide on, make it as ritualistic as you can; that is, do the cleaning with feeling. I know of some who will bury the stones in the ground for twenty-four hours, with the intention of allowing Mother Nature to put the energy back into the crystals. Others put the stones into a glass of water and place it in the window overnight to allow the moon to shine on it. Others place the stones onto larger clusters of crystals to be energised. There's no 'right' or 'wrong' way, only 'your' way.

Connecting to a crystal
Once you've found your healing gemstone-crystal or your lucky talisman, your lucky charm or your birthstone, you have to connect with it.

Remember the story of Aladdin and his three wishes? In the story, you'll remember, the Genie in the lamp was obliged to give three wishes to whoever owned the lamp; it didn't matter to the Genie who made the wishes. So before Aladdin could get his three wishes, firstly he had to own the lamp, and secondly he had to rub the lamp.

Here's the point: do you think if, in real life, you had Aladdin's lamp, there would ever be a time when you wouldn't know where it was? It's the same with your crystal. If at any time you are asked where it is and you don't know, then you are not connected. I am always being asked, 'How do I know if I am connected?' and the easiest answer I have found over the years is this: if you lost your crystal and didn't know you'd lost it, then you were not connected.

Enjoy the journey – the journey is life.

Any information given in this book is not intended to be taken as a replacement for medical advice. If in any doubt, always consult a qualified doctor or therapist.

THE MYSTICAL A TO Z OF STONES.

Agate … The agate probably derives its name from the small river Achates in Sicily, but can be found in many places including Brazil, Madagascar and India. Its rich variations make it a beautiful, multi-faceted stone. A powerful healer, it restores body energy and eases stressful situations; gives courage and banishes fear; calms, and increases self-esteem. A stone for good health and fortune, it helps grounding and balance. A stabiliser.

Amazonite … the 'thinkers' stone. It aids creativity and improves self-worth. A confidence stone. It attracts money and success. A soothing stone; a giver of energy. Solid blue to turquoise, it works on the throat – the fifth Chakra. It inspires hope and is sometimes also called 'the hope stone'.

Amber … not a stone, but the fossilised resin of extinct pine trees. Good for the throat – the fifth Chakra. Worn by actors for good luck and a clear voice. Changes negative energy into positive and is often used as a lucky talisman. It helps the body to heal itself. It is calming, lifting heaviness and allowing happiness to shine through. It prolongs life with a clear mind.

Amethyst ... purple to dark violet, known by a variety of names: Bishop's Stone, Stone of Healing, of Peace, of Love. St. Valentine implied it was one of the best gifts between lovers. Aids creative thinking. Relieves insomnia when placed under the pillow. A powerful aid to spiritual awareness and healing. Helps with meditation, inspiration, intuition and divine love. A stone which helps to attract that special partner.

Apache Tears ... a variant of Obsidian, dark, smokey, translucent in colour. Good for grounding; transforms; aids in the release of deep emotions. Eases pain, loss and sadness. Neutralises negative magic.

Apatite ... blue in colour. Strengthens muscle tissue, aids co-ordination, assists with stuttering and hypertension, and helps to fight viruses. Can help with communications, especially after a misunderstanding.

Aquamarine ... a Beryl, clear blue-green. It represents an ocean of love. Preserves innocence, brings spiritual vision, calms the mind and lifts the spirits, releases anxiety and fear. It is recommended for those suffering a lot of grief. Gives insight and perception in dealings with people. Gives protection, often used as a good luck charm. Leads to greater self-knowledge, quickens the mind, and promotes clear and logical thinking.

Aventurine ... a variety of Quartz, usually green with mica inclusions. Stabilises by inspiring independence, well-being and health. Acts as a general tonic on the physical level. If left in water overnight, it can be used to bathe the eyes, and similarly to treat skin irritations. Encourages creativity, gives courage, independence, calms and serenity. It is a money magnet and a good luck stone, a lucky talisman.

Azurite ... deep blue to blue-purple. An aid for meditation, it is used to increase psychic powers as it helps to induce prophetic dreams, intuition and understanding. It's also known as the 'Decision Maker'. With its high copper content it assists the flow of energy throughout the nervous system, strengthens the blood and is used to treat arthritis and joint disabilities.

Beryl ... many colours. The best of the Beryl group are emeralds and aquamarines. In ancient rituals the Beryl was used to bring rain. It is related to the sea and guards its wearer against drowning and sea-sickness. Protects against 'mind games'. Helps to stimulate the mind, and increases confidence. In the sixteenth century, it was worn to win arguments and debates.

Bloodstone (Heliotrope) ... a form of Jasper – dark green in colour, with red flecks. The red flecks are symbolic of Christ's death and his blood spilling onto the stone. Acts on all of the Chakras, a physical healer and a mental balancer. Removes toxins and aligns energies, especially along the spinal cord. Helps prevent miscarriages and eases childbirth. Works to overcome depression and pain of the emotional kind. Calming, grounding and revitalising. A stone to attract wealth, often used in business or legal matters to help attract success.

Calcite ... red, orange, yellow, green and blue (see the Chakras). There is also a clear variety of calcite called Iceland Spar which, when placed over a line on a piece of paper, will produce a double image. Calcite is a strong balancing stone, giving comfort and lifting depression. Also alleviates fear, aids mental clarity, calms turbulent emotions, expands awareness and aids intuition. Good for pancreas and spleen. Clears toxins by gently helping to cleanse the blood.

Carnelian (Cornelian) ... mainly bright orange. The 'friendly one' – it is a very highly evolved healer. A good balancer; can help you connect with your inner self. Good for concentration. Brings joy, sociability and warmth. Good for rheumatism, arthritis, depression, neuralgia, and helps to regularise the menstrual cycle. When coupled with amethyst, purifies consciousness, reverses negative thoughts and shakes off sluggishness.

Cat's Eye ... golden to mid-yellow, green to bluish brown. The Greeks called it 'Cymophane' meaning 'wave-light'. It resembles the contracted pupil of a cat's eye. In the symbolic necklace of 'Vishnu' the green gem was held to represent the earth. A magnetic centre of human passions. It is used to increase beauty and wealth, to protect, and to guard against danger.

Celestite ... white to clear; light blue cluster crystals. Signifies honesty. Helps with tiredness, soothes nerves and stress. Quietens the mind, promotes compassion, expands creative expression, reveals truth.

Chalcedony ... soft blue, translucent, belonging to a large group of crystalline forms and geodes. Stimulates optimism and enhances spiritual creativity. Diminishes nightmares and fear of the dark. A stone that guards travellers, and helps grounding through negative times. Banishes fear, mental illness, hysteria and depression.

Chrysocolla ... blue to blue-green opaque mineral, essentially a copper-element mineral. ' The women's friend', relieving tension, pains and problems, soothing period pains and pre-menstrual tension. Increases energy, wisdom and peace of mind. Alleviates feelings of guilt, clears all negativity and brings about patience and contentment. Helps to attract love.

Chrysoprase ... an apple-green form of chalcedony, the colour being due to traces of nickel. For wisdom and meditation. Helps the wearer to see clearly into personal problems, especially sexual frustrations and depressions. Worn to lift emotions, attract friends and shield against negativity.

Citrine ... clear to yellow-orange. Natural Citrine was originally amethyst, transformed by being reheated and burnt in the earth's crust. Helps to clear mental and emotional problems and improve memory. Enhances willpower, optimism and confidence. Helps those who feel they have lost their way in life and need to find a new sense of direction. Strengthens the immune system, improves poor circulation and aids tissue regeneration. Placing a single crystal or cluster into a safe, till or cash box helps to attract ever-increasing financial income.

Copper ... mixes easily with other metals; for example, copper, tin and zinc make bronze. Copper is thought to be one of the best transmitters of healing energy. This may be because it has been used very successfully against cholera; and that wearing copper improves the metabolism, reduces inflammation and increases blood flow. Worn next to the skin it soothes arthritis and rheumatism and can kill all kinds of bacteria. Certain bacteria are found in plenty on silver coins but are said never to be found on copper.

Coral ... red, pink or white. Calcium calcite was once a living sea creature and is therefore thought to contain 'life essence'. It is used as a protector, especially to safeguard children. Sometimes referred to as the 'Tree of Life of the Ocean', it protects and strengthens the wearer's emotional foundation. Also, because it symbolises fertility, it offers a defence against sterility.

Diamond ... a well-known mineral, the purest and hardest substance in nature. It forms the neatest and sharpest of all known cutting edges and is now used in microsurgery with spectacular effect. When used with loving, clear intent, it clears blockages and opens the crown Chakra. Amplifies the full spectrum of energies in the mind, body and spirit.

Diotase ... deep blue to green. Rivals the Emerald in its beauty and holistic healing powers. It empowers the heart with new depth, strength, healthiness, courage, and the ability to love deeply again. Promotes genuine, sincere emotional balance, self-worth and deep well-being; helps heal sadness, heartache, abuse and neglect. A stone for the heart.

Emerald ... green. An excellent general healer, used in ancient times as a blood detoxifier and anti-poison. Improves creativity, imagination, memory and quick-wittedness. Helps the intellect and improves intelligence. Gives power to see the future. Grants success in business ventures and offers patience, harmony, peace and prosperity. An emotional stabiliser.

Fluorite (Fluorspar) ... appears in all rainbow colours. A 'new age' stone that strengthens thought and balances mental energy. Good for meditation. Fluorite clears the mind of stress and aids sleep. Helps physical and mental healing and strengthens bone tissue, especially tooth enamel. Relieves dental disease, viral inflammations and pneumonia.

Garnet ... black, pink-red, yellow-brown, orange or green. A member of a vast gemstone family. A 'knight in shining armour', contains a little of most metals but especially aluminium, silicon and oxygen. A revitalising tonic for the whole body, creating a shield of positive energy; aids in dreams, past lives, self-confidence and personal courage, and attracts love.

Geodes ... are hollow volcanic bubbles containing crystals. All Quartz, Rock Crystal, Amethysts and Opal is formed within geodes. The effect is brought about by the mineral-rich watery fluids percolating into the cavity or hole left by the 'bubble' which occurred in the steaming red hot volcanic lava. Some geodes are huge enough to drive cars through, while others are small enough to fit in the palm of your hand.

Hematite ... a natural ferric oxide, a silver-grey metallic mirror-like stone. You either like or dislike it, there's no 'in between'. To those who like it, it's a very optimistic inspirer of courage and personal magnetism. It lifts gloominess and depression and, when used in conjunction with Carnelian, can prevent fatigue. Good for blood, spleen and generally strengthens the body. Effective during pregnancy; helps with stress.

Jade ... comes in a variety of colours. It's a money magnet, a good luck talisman, and a protector from accidents, evil spirits and bad luck. It encourages long life, safe journeys, wisdom, courage, peace and harmony. The geological term for Jade is Nephrite, from the Greek word 'nephros' meaning 'kidney'. As a healer, Jade is good for kidneys, bladder, lungs and heart; the immune system, and even high blood pressure.

Jasper ... chalcedony quartz. Multi-coloured. A popular talisman, well liked amongst psychic healers. Protects from all kinds of ailments. It's a powerful healing stone, invigorating and stabilising. It calms troubled minds and helps to slow down the ageing process. Helps those suffering from emotional problems by balancing the physical and emotional needs.

Jet ... a black glass-like substance – fossilised wood, another type of coal, mainly from Whitby in England. Even the Jet used in ancient Mesopotamia was thought to have been originally mined in Whitby. Like amber, when rubbed it becomes electrically charged. A good travel aid. Helps increased psychic awareness, guards against witchcraft, demons, melancholy and anxiety, and is very good for manic-depressives.

Kunzite ... pink to dark lilac-rose. Has a high lithium content. Named after Dr G F Kunz, a noted mineralogist. Good for both the emotional and spiritual heart; reduces depression and mood swings. When held, induces relaxation by releasing tension and stress. A balancer for mind, body and spirit. Benefits those with any kind of compulsive behaviour.

Kynite ... light blue. Contains aluminium. It is softer, lengthways than it is across, and is immune to the forces of other chemicals (such as acids). Brings out our natural ability to manifest things into reality via thoughts and visualisation. Encourages devotion, truth, loyalty and reliability.

Labradorite ... 'iridescent Feldspar'. Yellow, pink, green, blue and violet. When in trouble and in doubt, wear a Labradorite. A stone for today, it opens the energy flow to any or all of the Chakra centres, whichever is in greatest need. Brings restful sleep and straightening of the spine.

Lapis Lazuli ... medium to dark blue with gold pyrite flecks. Called by the ancient Egyptians 'the Stone of Heaven', and thought to be the stone upon which were carved the laws given to Moses. A stone for teachers; helps ease expression and gain higher wisdom and Clarity.

Lapis Lazuli cont. ...
Good for mental, physical, spiritual, psychic and emotional problems, and well-known for healing the whole. Alleviates fear and eases depression, quiets the mind; helps with creativity, writing, dreams, insight, self-expression and finding inner truth.

Malachite ... dark and light bands of green tints. Its name probably comes from the Greek 'malache' ('mallow', as of the colour of a green mallow leaf). Egyptians used green Malachite paste for eye make-up. Stimulates physical and psychic vision and concentration. Contains copper and is useful in treating rheumatism and arthritis. Good for raising the spirits, increasing health, hope and happiness. Brings prosperity and is used to guard against all negativity.

Moldavite ... formed by a meteorite strike in the Moldau Valley area of the Czech Republic over twelve million years ago. A powerful healing stone, it helps telepathic access to spiritual laws, and attracts information from higher levels to help us and our earth to become healthier and more spiritual. Helps us to understand our true purpose in life. A stone of transformation.

Moonstone ... an opalescent Feldspar. In India the Moonstone is a sacred gem, thought to be lucky if given by the groom to his bride. Called the 'travellers' stone because it was a favourite protective amulet for those going on perilous journeys. Claimed to promote long life and happiness. It soothes stress and anxiety and is good for period pains and other kindred disorders. A powerful fertility and good luck stone from India.

Mother of Pearl ... is the lustrous, opalescent interior of various sea molluscs. Aptly dubbed the 'sea of tranquillity', it creates physical harmony of a gentle but persuasive kind. Calms the nerves. Indicates treasure, chastity, sensitivity and strength. Good for calcified joints and the digestive system. Relaxes and soothes the emotions; helps with sensitivity and stress. Carries the gentle, peaceful healing energy of the sea.

Obsidian Snowflake ... not really a stone, but a volcanic glass. Also Obsidian Black, Mahogany and clear. For all those it recognises, it's a powerful healer. Keeps energy well grounded, clears subconscious blocks and brings an insight and understanding of the power behind silence, detachment, wisdom and love. A very lucky talisman, a bringer of good fortune. Was favoured by ancient Mexican cultures to neutralise negative energy and black magic. Good for eyesight, stomach and intestines.

Onyx ... black, 'lightweight' Quartz. It can give a sense of courage and help to discover truth. Instils calm and serenity; diminishes depression. Gives self-control whilst aiding detachment and inspiring serenity. A protective stone worn in times of conflict, a student's friend as it encourages concentration and protects against unwise decisions. It is often found in rosaries; it helps to improve devotion, and relieves stress.

Opal ... a silica. The 'Rainbow Stone'. Multi-coloured, it is a wonderful stone to behold, and can be charged with virtually every type of energy needed. It controls temper and calms the nerves. It was sometimes considered unlucky, but (according to Thomas Nichols' book of 1652) this is probably why: 'Opalus:-cloudeth the eyes of those that stand about him who wears it, so that they can either not see or not mind what is done before them; for this cause it is asserted to be a safe patron of thieves and thefts.' Because of its beauty, things were stolen or went missing, hence, according to some, its unlucky label.

Peridot ... clear bright green, also green to yellow (Chrysolite). A good anti-toxin gem, for cleaning most organs and glands. An overall tonic. Used by the Egyptians, Aztecs and Incas to gently help cleanse and heal the physical, including heart, lungs, lymph and muscles. Prized by the Crusaders as 'their' stone. It clears energy pathways, strengthens the 'breath of life', and attracts prosperity, growth and openness. It's also useful for attracting love and opening new doors of opportunity and abundance.

Rhodocrosite ... a solid to clear, beautiful pink stone. Good for giving and receiving love. Inspires forgiveness. Heals emotional scars; helps to cope with loneliness, loss, heartache, fears, insecurities and inner child issues. Helps prevent mental breakdown and balances physical and emotional traumas. Soothes and de-stresses the body, cheers the depressed and coaxes back the life force in the very sick.

Rhodonite ... pink with black inclusions. Improves memory, calms the mind and reduces stress. Gives confidence and self-esteem. Cheers the depressed, preserves youth and retards the aging process. Helps to bring back the life force into the sick. Carries the power to the unobstructed love. Good for emotional trauma, mental breakdown, spleen, kidneys, heart and blood circulation. A very special stone.

Rock Crystal ... also known traditionally as Clear Quartz. This stone holds a place of unique importance in the world of gems. It enlarges the aura of everything near to it, by acting as a catalyst to increase the healing powers of other minerals. Its vibration resonates with the beat of life, giving Rock Crystal a key role in all holistic practices. Good for the mind and soul, strengthening, cleansing and protecting, especially against negativity.

Rose Quartz ... translucent to clear pink. Possesses healing qualities for the mind. It can help with migraine and headaches. It excites the imagination, helps to release pent-up emotions, lifts spirits and dispels negative thoughts. Eases both emotional and sexual imbalances and increases fertility. Good for spleen, kidneys and circulatory system. Coupled with Hematite, works wonders on aches and pains throughout the whole body.

Ruby ... blood red. Plays a vital role in micro-surgery as a cauterising instrument. Used to alleviate all kinds of blood disorders, anaemia, poor circulation, heart disease, rheumatism and arthritis. Helps ease worries; lifts the spirits. Improves confidence, intuition and spiritual wisdom, courage and energy; produces joy, dispels fear and strengthens willpower. Gives strength in leadership and success over challengers.

Rutilated Quartz ... clear Quartz which contains titanium oxide in the form of slender needles; these amplify the energy of the Quartz. It aids healing, eases bronchial problems and increases tissue growth. Also stimulates mental activity and eases depression, improves decisiveness, strength of will, and helps to communicate with the higher self.

Sapphire ... related to Ruby. A range of colours, but best known and loved for the dark blue variety. Worn to stimulate the 'third eye', to expand wisdom during meditation. A sacred gem worn by kings to ward off evil. Good for improving the state of mind, increasing clarity of thought and dispelling confusion. Calms the nerves, attracts good influences and strengthens faith. Reputed to lengthen life, keeping its wearers looking young. Fortifies the heart and is a guardian of love, feelings and emotions.

Smokey Quartz ... looks exactly as its name implies – smokey. A grounding stone. Ideal around electrical goods such as computers, because it disperses negative patterns and vibrations. It can draw out and absorb negative energies, replacing them with positive.

Smokey Quartz cont....
Alleviates moods, depression and other negative emotions; protects against despair, grief and anger. Used in meditation, it helps explore the inner self by penetrating dark areas with light and love. A 'Dream Stone'.

Sodalite ... deep blue with veined white flecks; often mistaken for Lapis Lazuli, but lacks the golden flecks. Calms and clears the mind, enhancing communication and insight with higher self. A good stone for people who are over-sensitive and defensive. Brings joy and relieves a heavy heart. When placed at the side of the bed it can make a sad person wake up full of the joys of spring. Imparts youth and freshness to its wearer. When coupled with Rhodonite it produces the 'Elixir of Life'.

Tiger Eye ... generally associated with yellow to chocolate-brown. An iridescent combination of colour, resembling the gleaming eye of a tiger at night. The stone has a shifting lustre of golden light across it. Inspires brave but sensible behaviour with great insight and clear perception. Fights hypochondria and psychosomatic diseases. A true 'confidence stone'. It attracts good luck, protects from witchcraft, and is an ideal 'worry stone' (let the stone do the worrying). Always carry one for protection.

Topaz ... many different colours, the most popular being rose-red to pure white. Named after the island Topazion. Known as the 'abundant one'; a stone of strength; a charm against fires and accidents. Promotes good health by overcoming stress, depression, exhaustion, fears and worries. Good for soothing, tranquillising, calming and protecting.

Tourmaline ... has a colour for all seven of the Chakras. A master physician from the mineral world, working on all Chakra levels. A strong protector against misfortune and misunderstandings, it attracts goodwill, love and friendships. It settles troubled minds, gives confidence, inspires, calms the nerves, expands mental energy and helps clarity of thought.

Turquoise ... an opaque, light blue to green mineral. A sacred stone to native American Indians, and a powerful talisman to the Egyptians and the Turkish. A Lucky Stone, a protector against radiation and dark forces; a talisman favoured by horse-riders. A good all-round general healer, gentle, cooling and soothing; a stone that brings wisdom and psychic connection to the Universal Spirit. Turquoise strengthens and aligns all Chakras and energy fields. An absorber of negativity, a guardian against failure and poverty.

Unikite ... usually green with red patches. A variety of granite. Its name is taken from the Unaka range of mountains in North Carolina, USA. Autumnal in colour, it is a beautiful stone. It helps the wearer to relax and find peace of mind. It works mainly on a higher plain rather than the physical, going beyond into the spiritual world to find truth, bringing an understanding the true cause of disease and discomfort.

Zircon ... from the Arabic word 'Zarkun' ('vermilion'). Similar to diamond in lustre and colour and often used as a substitute for diamonds. Known as the 'Stone of Virtue', it strengthens the mind and brings joy to the heart. Represents vitality, and works with the 'crown' Chakra, helping to connect to Universal truth. Good for intuition, integrity, insomnia and depression.

oOo

A SPECIAL GLOSSARY OF HEALING STONES

You may believe it's God's Power, or brought about by a Universal Life force, or just simply derived from a natural state of 'evolution'. I believe that the power to 'heal' can be found within the mind, and more importantly in the 'imagination', especially when it's coupled with a 'feeling'.

The following lists have been specially compiled into 'Combinations' of either two or three Gemstones and Crystals rather than single stones. When used correctly 'Combinations' can have very powerful, positive effects within the mind.

Precautionary Warning:
*Please remember the following information **is not authoritative**, but is a fluid interpretation drawn from many sources. It is always advisable to consult your own Doctor before embarking on any course of self-treatment or using any type of alternative therapy.*

NB: On no account should a gemstone or Crystal ever be swallowed.

A

Aches & Pains (easing of)	Rose Quartz, Rock Crystal & Hematite
Abdominal Colic	Mother of Pearl & Obsidian Snowflake
Accidents (prevention of)	Yellow Carnelian & Tiger Eye
Addiction	Amethyst & Black Onyx
Adults Only (aphrodisiac)	Rose Quartz, Amethyst & Carnelian
Acidity	Green Jasper & Rock Crystal
Ageing (to retard general process of)	'Elixir of Life' Sodalite & Rhodonite
Aggression (moderation of)	Carnelian & Amethyst
Alcoholism	Amethyst & Black Onyx
Allergies	Red Jasper, Rock Crystal & Carnelian
Anaemia	Citrine & Hematite
Anger	Carnelian & Amethyst
Angina	Rose Quartz & Amethyst
Animals (to cure illnesses)	Rose Quartz & Rock Crystal
Anorexia	Rhodocrosite & Rose Quartz
Anxiety	Rock Crystal & Tiger Eye
Arthritis	Mother of Pearl & Carnelian
	Also Copper & Magnets
Asthma	Amber & Rose Quartz

B

Backache	Blue agate & Hematite
Bad Temper	Blue tiger Eye & Green Aventurine
Baldness	Aquamarine & Rock Crystal
Bladder	Jade & Red Jasper
Bleeding	Bloodstone & Carnelian
Blood Circulation	Sodalite & Carnelian
Blood Pressure (high)	Jade & Sodalite
Blood Pressure (low)	Sodalite & Carnelian
Brain Tonic	Amethyst & Carnelian
Breathlessness	Amber & Black Onyx
Bronchitis	Amber & Black Onyx

Bruises	Rose Quartz & Carnelian
Burns	Sodalite & Amethyst

C

Calming	Sodalite & Rock Crystal
Cancer	Red Jasper, Rock Crystal & Carnelian
Catarrh	Amber & Blue Agate
Cell Rejuvenation	Sodalite & Rhodonite
Central Nervous System	Rock Crystal & Rose Quartz
Chest Pains	Malachite & Rose Quartz
Circulation	Sodalite & Carnelian
Concentration	Carnelian & Red Jasper
Constipation	Red Jasper & Citrine
Coughs	Aquamarine & Blue Agate
Courage	Hematite & Tiger Eye
Cramp	Bloodstone & Amethyst
Creativity	Amethyst & Red Jasper
Crown Energy	Rock Crystal & Amethyst

D

Depression (to lift)	Tiger Eye, Carnelian & Hematite
Despair	Rhodonite & Carnelian
Diabetes	Rock Crystal & Red Jasper
Digestion	Citrine & Obsidian Snowflake
Dreams	Rutilated Quartz & Jade
Drunkenness	Amethyst & Tiger Eye

E

Ear Problems	Amethyst & Blue Agate
Eczema	Amethyst & Green Aventurine
Elixir of Life	Rhodonite & Sodalite
Emotional Strength	Amethyst & Rose Quartz
Energy Booster	Amethyst, Rock Crystal & Carnelian
Epilepsy	Black Onyx & Tourmaline
Eyesight	Obsidian Snowflake & Rose Quartz

F

Fainting	Amethyst & Lapis Lazuli
Fatigue	Amethyst, Rock Crystal & Carnelian
Fear	Rose Quartz & Rhodonite
Fertility	Rock Crystal, Rose Quartz & Moonstone
Fever	Carnelian & Red Jasper
Forgetfulness	Rhodonite & Unakite
Fractures	Mother of Pearl & Hematite
Frustration	Obsidian Clear & Rose Quartz

G

Gall Bladder	Red Jasper & Tiger Eye
General Tonic	Green Aventurine & Blue Agate
Good Luck	Moonstone, Green Aventurine & Obsidian Snowflake
Grief	Red Jasper & Obsidian Clear

H

Haemorrhoids	Mother of Pearl & Obsidian Clear
Hair	Aquamarine & Rock Crystal
Happiness	Carnelian & Sodalite
Hay Fever	Amber & Tiger Eye
Headache	Rose Quartz & Hematite
Hearing	Blue Agate & Rhodonite
Heart Disease	Rock Crystal, Red Jasper & Carnelian
Hypochondria	Tiger Eye & Blue Agate

I

Imagine (a key to Life)	Rose Quartz, Green Aventurine & Amethyst
Immune System	Blue Agate & Carnelian
Impotence	Rhodonite & Sodalite
Indigestion	Jasper & Citrine
Insomnia	Amethyst & Sodalite

Intestine	Mother of Pearl & Obsidian Snowflake
Intuition	Amethyst & Rock Crystal
Irritated Throat	Amber & Rhodonite
Itching	Green Aventurine & Hematite

K

Kidney	Jade & Carnelian
Knees	Mother of Pearl & Blue Agate
Knowledge	Amethyst & Rock Crystal

L

Laryngitis	Amber & Rhodonite
Laziness	Hematite & Blue Agate
Liver	Rhodonite & Jasper
Loneliness	Rhodochrosite & Amethyst
Longevity	Sodalite & Rhodonite
Love (potion)	Rose Quartz & Amethyst
Lungs	Fluorite & Amber

M

Melancholy	Red Jasper & Carnelian
Memory	Rhodonite & Unakite
Menopause	Moonstone & Rose Quartz
Menstrual Cycle	Carnelian & Moonstone
Migraine	Rose Quartz & Obsidian Clear
Mouth	Sodalite & Tiger Eye
Multiple Sclerosis	Red Jasper, Rock Crystal & Carnelian
Muscles	Rock Crystal & Hematite

N

Nails	Rhodochrosite & Mother of Pearl
Neck	Hematite & Rose Quartz
Negative Energy (to dispel)	Lapis Lazuli & Obsidian Snowflake
Nervousness	Rhodonite & Mother of Pearl

Neuralgia	Rose Quartz & Hematite
Nightmares	Amethyst & Rhodonite

O

Obesity	Black Onyx & Rock Crystal
Obsessions	Blue Agate & Black Onyx

P

Pain (to relieve)	Rose Quartz, Rock Crystal & Hematite
Paralysis	Amethyst & Rock Crystal
Patience	Rock Crystal & Howlite
Peace of Mind	Green Aventurine, Rose Quartz & Rhodonite
Phobias	Obsidian Clear & Rose Quartz
Pregnancy (for strength)	Hematite & Carnelian
Prosperity	Green Aventurine & Obsidian Snowflake
Protection	Tiger Eye & Obsidian Snowflake
Public Speaking	Amber & Tiger Eye

Q

Quarrelling (between couples)	Rose quartz, Green Aventurine & Rhodonite

R

Red Blood Cells (to promote health)	Hematite & Amethyst
Rejuvenator	Sodalite & Rhodonite
Reproductive System	Rose Quartz & Moonstone
Rheumatism	Mother of Pearl & Carnelian

S

Sadness	Sodalite & Red Jasper
Scar Tissue	Rose Quartz & Rock Crystal
Sciatica	Rose Quartz & Hematite

Serenity	Rock Crystal & Rhodonite
Sexual Appetite (to arouse)	Rose Quartz, Amethyst & Carnelian
Shyness	Tiger Eye & Hematite
Sinus	Sodalite & Black Onyx
Skin Problems	Green Aventurine & Rose Quartz
Sleep	Amethyst & Howlite
Smell (to improve sense of)	Red Jasper & Tiger Eye
Sores	Green Aventurine & Amethyst
Speech	Rhodonite & Blue Agate
Stamina	Amethyst, Rock Crystal & Carnelian
Stomach	Mother of Pearl & Obsidian Snowflake
Stress	Green Aventurine, Rose Quartz & Rhodonite

T

Teeth	Mother of Pearl & Calcite
Tension	Rose Quartz & Carnelian
Throat	Blue Agate & Amber
Thyroid	Rhodonite & Lapis Lazuli
Tiredness	Amethyst, Rose Quartz & Carnelian
Tumours	Amethyst & Rose Quartz

U

Ulcers	Green Aventurine & Tiger Eye
Urinary System	Citrine & Jade

V

Varicose Veins	Aquamarine & Rhodonite
Vertigo	Red Jasper & Obsidian Clear
Vocal Cords	Rhodonite & Blue Agate

W

Wasting Disease	Red Jasper, Rock Crystal & Carnelian
Weak muscles	Amethyst, Rock Crystal & Hematite

Weakness (general)	Amethyst, Rock Crystal & Hematite
Will Power	Rose Quartz, Black Onyx & Rock Crystal
Wisdom	Amethyst & Carnelian
Wounds	Rose Quarts & Rock Crystal

oOo

Look at things not as they are, but as they can be. You can accomplish almost anything if you believe you can. We all have God-given talents and abilities, if only we can learn how to use them.

Keep an open mind … for many, Crystal Healing works and has proved to be very beneficial, so discover for yourself if you can be one of those people.

If thinking is the rocket
then believing is the propellant

If thinking is the birth of the desire
then believing makes the connection to the
'Power' that makes it happen

Birthstones

On the next page you will find my list of twelve Birthstones. In my research I studied over seventeen different lists. My list is the same as the Bibles list for Aries, Virgo and Pisces. These lists have been well researched. There are many others. However, I believe the first list to be authentic. The second list gives the most popular precious stones for the United Kingdom; and the third list is taken from the bible: a 'New Jerusalem'.

Birthstones can act as Lucky Talismans. The function of a talisman is to make possible the powerful transformations which a person would not normally feel empowered to do without a little extra help.

Although there's no basis in science for luck and maybe luck is only an illusion of control, but control is what we try to seek in a random world.

Lucky talismans, charms and amulets can give a sense of preparedness, a feeling of control and a more positive outlook on life, which in itself may give us that 'edge', an extra push to help improve our life, and change it for the better.

Birthstones

Zodiac Star signs	Semi-precious Stones	Precious Stones	Bible Rev. 21-19
Aries (21 Mar. – 20 Apr.)	Red Jasper	Diamond	Jasper
Taurus (21 Apr. – 21 May)	Rose Quartz	Emerald	Sapphire
Gemini (22 May – 21 Jun.)	Black Onyx	Pearl	Chalcedony
Cancer (22 Jun. – 22 Jul.)	Mother of Pearl	Ruby	Emerald
Leo (23 Jul. – 23 Aug.)	Tiger Eye	Peridot	Sardonyx
Virgo (24 Aug. – 22 Sep.)	Carnelian	Sapphire	Carnelian
Libra (23 Sep. – 23 Oct.)	Green Aventurine	Opal	Chroysolite
Scorpio (24 Oct. – 22 Nov.)	Rhodonite	Topaz	Beryl
Sagittarius (23 Nov. -21 Dec.)	Sodalite	Turquoise	Topaz
Capricorn (22 Dec. – 20 Jan.)	Obsidian Snowflake	Garnet	Chrysoprase
Aquarius (21 Jan. – 19 Feb.)	Blue Agate	Amethyst	Jacinth
Pisces (20 Feb. – 20 Mar.)	Amethyst	Aquamarine	Amethyst

oOo

Always use your wisdom – the ability to think and act utilising knowledge, experience, understanding, common sense and insight.

According to the teachings of the Holy Quran:
The Universal Life Force, the maker and sustainer of the world, the creator of and provider for man, the Active Force and Effective Power in Nature are all one and the same, known to some as Allah and to others as God. This is the secret of all secrets and the most supreme of all beings.

Belief in God and His great power alone can provide mankind with the best possible explanation of many mysterious things in life. This is the safest way to true knowledge and spiritual insight, the right path to good behaviour and sound morals, the surest guide to happiness and prosperity.

And finally…
In this world of uncertainties you will, as you travel along your journey through life, discover that not everything goes quite according to plan. At these times in our lives it's often reassuring to realise that deep down within the very heart of our souls, we know that there's more to this life than meets the eye, and that reaching out through the mysteries of life we all have our own guides, our angels helping us through. We are part of creation, just as Gemstones and Crystals are. We are all connected to the universe; by looking beyond our world we will in time realise that the things which we seek outside, we already have within.

Gemstones and Crystals are tools to help to connect to that which we desire. It's like making a phone call to a helpline: the Gemstones and Crystals are the phone, we do the dialling and the asking, and then we hope that the Universal Life Force can, and will help.

If you are having difficulty obtaining any of the stones mentioned in this book, we do offer our own mail order service and would be more than pleased to supply any of the stones listed. We also have our 'themed' "Power for Life – Power Bracelets" based on and around this book. All details on our web site:-

www.rosewood-gifts.co.uk

INDEX

PART ONE

INDEX

Other titles in the 'POWER FOR LIFE' series of mini-books:-

Discover your own Special Birthstone and the renowned Healing Powers of Crystals REF. (BK1) A look at Birthstones, personality traits and characteristics associated with each Sign of the Zodiac – plus a guide to the author's own unique range of Power Gems.

A Special Glossary of Healing Stones plus Birthstones REF. (BK2) An Introduction to Crystal Healing, with an invaluable Glossary listing common ailments and suggesting combinations of Gemstones and Crystals.

Create a Wish Kit using a Candle, a Crystal and the Imagination of your Mind REF. (BK3) 'The key to happiness is having dreams; the key to success is making your dreams come true'. This book will help you to achieve.

Gemstone & Crystal Elixirs – Potions for Love, Health, Wealth, Energy and Success REF. (BK4) An ancient form of 'magic', invoking super-natural powers. You won't believe the power you can get from a drink!

Crystal Pendulum for Dowsing REF (BK5) An ancient knowledge for unlocking your Psychic Power, to find out information not easily available by any other means. Contains easy-to-follow instructions.

Crystal Healing – Fact or Fiction? Real or Imaginary? REF (BK6) Find the answer in this book. Discover a hidden code used by Jesus Christ for Healing, and read about the science of light and colour. It's really amazing.

How to Activate the Hidden Power in Gemstones and Crystals REF (BK7) The key is to energise the thought using a crystal. The conscious can direct – but discover the real power. It's all in this book.

Astrology: The Secret Code REF (BK8) In church it's called 'Myers Briggs typology'. In this book it's called 'psychological profiling'. If you read your horoscope, you need to read this to find your true birthstone.

Talismans, Charms and Amulets REF (BK9) Making possible the powerful transformations which we would normally feel empowered to do without a little extra help. Learn how to make a lucky talisman.

A Guide to the Mysteries surrounding Gemstone & Crystals REF (BK10) Crystal healing, birthstones, crystal gazing, lucky talismans, elixirs, crystal dowsing, astrology, rune stones, amulets and rituals.

A Simple Guide to Gemstone & Crystal Power – a mystical A-Z of stones REF (BK11) From Agate to Zircon, all you ever needed or wanted to know about the Mystical powers of gemstones and crystals.

Change your Life by using the Most Powerful Crystal on Earth REF (BK12) The most powerful crystal on earth can be yours. A book so disarmingly simple to understand, yet with a tremendous depth of Knowledge.

All the above books are available on Kindle
Or, from the publisher www.rosewood-gifts.co.uk

Welcome to the world of Rosewood Gifts/Publishing

If you like natural products, hand-crafted gifts
including Gemstone jewellery, objects of natural
beauty – the finest examples from Mother Nature, tinged
with an air of Mystery – then we hope you will not be disappointed.
For those who can enjoy that feeling of connection with the
esoteric nature of Gemstones and Crystals, then our 'Themed'
"Power for Life" – Power Bracelets could be ideal for you.

Each bracelet comes with its own guide explaining
'How to Activate the Hidden Power
in Gemstones and Crystals'

We regularly give inspirational "Power for Life" seminars.
Presented by Robert W Wood D.Hp
**For like minds wanting to find Peace and Harmony in
Mind, Body and Spirit**
A captivating story about the world's fascination with natural
Gemstones and Crystals, often described as both intriguing
and electrifying,
but never disappointing.

To see our full range of books, jewellery and gifts

Visit our web site – www.rosewood-gifts.co.uk

To see our latest videos go to 'You Tube'
And type in Rosewood Gifts.

Printed in the USA
CPSIA information can be obtained
at www.ICGtesting.com
LVHW020847080124
R18021200005B/R180212PG767912LVX00026B/35

9 780956 791320